PUNCHING ABOVE YOUR WEIGHT

The untold story of the martial arts

liamdevonport.com
@LiamDevonportAuthor

Also by Liam Devonport

Zenith: The Science, History and Mythology of the Northern Lights*

*Zenith achieved Amazon's #1 New Release accolade in two categories (Arctic and Antarctic History & History of Astronomy)

To Roxana – Hubco

To Isla – Welcome to the world!

To Simba – Woof woof!

Praise for *Punching Above Your Weight*

'As a former student of mine, Liam was diligent, hardworking, and focussed on being the best martial artist he could be. He's now transferred those skills over into his writing. This book, I believe, will benefit both the experienced martial artist and the novice who is looking to take up a martial art for the first time and is wondering which one would be most suitable for them.'

**Mike Gregory, Instructor under Dan Inosanto
Jun Fan Gung Fu/Filipino Martial Arts**

'A comprehensive overview of different martial arts styles, their philosophy and historical routes and their evolution over time. Liam journeys with the reader across the globe to uncover the principles and delves into the techniques that make each style unique as well as showing their lineage to an original form and origin. This book gives a real taste of global martial arts and an insight into which might just be the route for you. A roundhouse of a book that packs a real punch!'

**David Ochwat
Kickboxing Blackbelt**

AS FEATURED

UK Martial Arts Show

MALMAG (Martial Arts Lifestyle Magazine)

Derbyshire Times

Around Saddleworth Magazine

Glossop Chronicle

First published in Great Britain

Liam Devonport asserts the moral right to be identified as the
author of this work.

ISBN: 9798391757719

Cover design by Jansen Lee

Cover image by Edward Eyer

Haiku by the author

Together we seek,

With body and mind in kind,

The truth of the arts.

Contents

'If size mattered then the elephant would be king of the jungle.'

Rickson Gracie

INTRODUCTION

Once upon a time, many moons ago, someone was punched in the face. Being punched in the face is never a pleasant experience – I'm not sure why I'm having to tell you this. I'm sure you already know, regardless of whether you've taken a fist to the nose or not. But this time, all those years ago, it was different. The person in question disliked taking a clenched fist to the nostrils so much, they decided to do whatever they could to stop it happening again. And in that moment of anger and frustration, as they regained their composure, and probably tried to pass it off as nothing to a group of curious spectators who pointed and smirked, the martial arts were born.

Martial arts are essentially a series of fighting techniques, movements, and philosophies (often referred to as styles) initially devised for the purposes of self-defence and combat. So, let's take our friend who has just been punched in the nose as an example. By vowing to never allow such an unwarranted atrocity to happen again, they would first have to analyse the scuffle in hindsight, apply logic, creativity, and physics to the situation, and then devise a way to counter such an instance occurring in the future. This in itself is a martial thought pattern. A series of trial and error, cause and effect, analysis of biomechanics and human mental and physical capability, and the hope of being able to kick someone else's ass in the process, instead of having yours kicked, again.

As you would imagine, as it is with all creative endeavours, some pursuits succeeded, and others, ironically, fell flat on their face. There are some atrocious martial arts out there you would be wasted studying. Unless, for some bizarre reason, you wanted to make yourself *less* effective in combat. And there are some even more appalling instructors; each of whom is doing the martial arts community a gross disservice by running what is effectively known as a 'McDojo' – a club of such hilarious ineptitude that its teachings are dangerous to the student and not the person attacking them. Some of these instructors promise the world whilst delivering ill-

1

conceived logic, theories, and techniques. They instil unjust confidence in their students whilst proffering half-baked thoughts and concepts. Examples abound, such as the ability to defeat an opponent with nothing more than the power of the mind. When these schools are tested in combat against real martial artists, they *always* fail. But they quickly put forward deluded excuses as to why their art didn't work in the name of self-preservation. But the real danger here is that many of these instructors truly believe their own bullshit.

On the flip side of the coin, however, there are some incredible martial arts in the world. Arts so capable that if you are not privy to their ways your mind would struggle to comprehend their effectiveness. It's simply amazing what the human body is capable of given time, tutelage, and opportunity. And to match these arts, there are some mind-numbingly proficient instructors, with the skills, knowledge, and experience to transform you from average Joe to fighting machine. It would be no exaggeration to state that if you picked a fight with an experienced martial artist from one of these styles (Brazilian Jiu Jitsu, for example) you would probably wake up from an unconscious spell without ever knowing how you got there.

There is little in this world that can bring together people from contrasting backgrounds, with different beliefs and mindsets, in a humbling and respectful manner. And as we shall see, the wisdom and vigour of martial arts can cross borders, unite cultures, and inspire people from all walks of life. The world could learn a lot from martial arts. In the words of Renzo Gracie, 'There's more philosophy in Jiu Jitsu mats than an Ivy League school in America.'

My journey into martial arts started more years ago than I care to admit. Let's just say we weren't even in the 21st century when I started, and there was no such thing as a smartphone. As with most, I was inspired by the prospect of flying kicks, big, grandiose techniques, monks in orange robes, and the ability to defeat multiple opponents without breaking sweat. In my mind, my future martial arts journey would take me to misty mountains, hidden dojos, long-bearded masters, mountain top temples, and Japanese bamboo forests. When in actuality, it took me to the local YMCA opposite a disused building site twice a week. Not quite what I had in mind. But, nevertheless, my journey had begun, and I would learn more about the arts and myself than I ever thought possible.

My style of choice was a Kung Fu Kickboxing hybrid. The first class I ever took was a juxtaposition of emotions. Firstly, I was more out of shape, less flexible, and supremely less talented than I imagined. I had good coordination (a gift I had always possessed which is beneficial in martial arts) but apart from that, I was talentless in my new environment. People half my size could beat me up. The higher grades could outwit me with one hand and their eyes closed – no joke. I was completely lost, even with the most basic of movements. And my instructor didn't have a long white beard that he stroked whilst he contemplated my inadequacy. It was a humbling experience. However, upon leaving that first class I have seldom felt more confident. I felt powerful, skilled, and dangerous. I felt I could defend myself against the most vociferous attacker, as long as they punched me slowly, and in the one position I had practiced in my first class. I was hooked, and I knew I would never look back.

I continued in pursuit of my blackbelt – the goal of every new martial artist. The blackbelt, up there on its pedestal, is the holy grail to beginner martial artists. Its darkness is enthralling, like a powerful amulet luring you in. You think that to have a blackbelt around your waist means you have conquered martial knowledge. And when you see the blackbelts move in class they are fluid, effortless, skilled, decisive, and purposeful in their actions. I hoped to be like them one day. And one day I was. Although when I achieved my blackbelt, I never felt like I was as good as the people who'd been blackbelts when I was a white belt. It's strange really, how you judge yourself differently from other people. How you are less inclined to believe in your own achievements than other people's. Looking back on the day I earned my blackbelt, all I can say is it was a rather underwhelming experience. As the years went by, I had incrementally gotten better, but I was never really aware of the leaps in improvement I had made. Because to me, the upskilling was day by day, making it much harder to track and recognise. I had expected a moment of awakening. A moment when all my hard work would pay off at once, but it never came. It happened with every kick, punch, and strike I threw, one move at a time. As I have come to realise about all things in life, it's not the moments of awakening or seismic change that define your achievements (these are few and far between and many of us only get a couple in a lifetime), it's the day in day out grind that makes the difference. The small incremental improvements we work towards each day. There is a Japanese name for this dedicated gradual improvement: Kaizen philosophy. Many people, not just martial artists, adopt Kaizen philosophy as a tried and tested route to success. But within a martial arts context, Kaizen philosophy's most famous proclamation comes from its most dedicated advocate, Bruce Lee, when he said, 'If you spend too much time thinking about a thing, you'll never get it done. Make at least one definite move daily towards your goal.' I had always been told by my instructor and other blackbelts, but never truly believed, 'a blackbelt is not the end of the journey, it's the beginning'. You only truly start to learn martial arts once you have achieved your blackbelt – and I can now attest to this being entirely true. I would actually go as far to say that belts don't even matter. Blue, green, yellow, purple brown, black, whatever. They don't mean anything. They are simply a way of letting you know how you're doing. I personally prefer to train without a belt-based grading system and just feel my improvements over time. This is what a blackbelt has taught me that sometimes what you think is an end is only the beginning.

Soon afterwards I took up Jeet Kune Do (JKD), which is philosophical martial concept devised by Bruce Lee. JKD was unlike anything I had experienced before. I had never imagined such ideas, concepts, and creativity could be amalgamated into a singl expression of fighting. JKD truly changed the way I looked at martial arts and my interpretation of what they meant, what they were, how they affect you as a person, and how they'd changed over the years. JKD gyms can vary greatly in their interpretation of its philosophy, as is the nature of JKD I suppose. The gym I trained at focussed on four main areas: Jun Fan Gung Fu (a style of Kung Fu devised by Bruce Lee), the Filipino martial arts, Muay Thai, and Combat Submission Wrestling (CSW). I found these four arts to be the perfect mix. Jun Fan Gung Fu provided punching, trapping, and kicking; the Filipino arts offered both empty hand and weapons training (sticks and knives); Muay Thai allowed me to work my clinching, knees, elbows, and kicks; and CSW provided a solid grappling and submission game.

This is not a book about Kung Fu, Kickboxing, or JKD, however, nor any singular art for that matter. It's a book that aims to look at the arts as a whole – including the grappling arts, which most books on this subject seem to omit. When the term 'martial arts' or 'arts' is used, for the purpose of this book it will refer to both martial arts and combat sports as a whole. Although combat sports and martial arts sometimes like to be separately classified, grouping them under the single term 'martial arts' will make our story easier to follow and understand. There will unavoidably be sections that orientate around specific arts, as it is impossible to talk about the whole without mentioning its constituent parts. But the idea is to look at the arts by starting in the past and working our way towards the future. I want to show how the arts have evolved over the years and see what lessons we can distil from that process. You shouldn't be concerned if you're not a martial artist, as I hope there will be much to take from this book regardless of your knowledge or experience. I will not be speaking in technical terms (but if there's anything you're not sure about you can refer to the Glossary), nor analysing techniques and movements in mind-numbing detail. I will be looking to the story of the arts, their beginnings, myths and legends, philosophies, science, evolution, societal influence, and future. I aim to tell a brief story of the arts that is fun, educational, and hopefully interesting. A story that only requires a transitory appreciation of the arts to enjoy.

We will start with their beginnings by looking at their history and place in the world. We will also investigate five of the most well-known martial arts to see where they came from, what they are, and how they're different from one another. After this we will look to see what the difference is between the *martial* and the *art*, and why they are both important to a martial artist's longevity. We will then investigate how the martial arts focus on three main areas: mind, body, and spirit; and how they aim to focus, hone, and develop each of these as the student progresses. There are thousands of martial arts in the world, each of which have their roots and origins in separate ideas, philosophies, and locations. As I'm sure you'll agree, it will be interesting to look at a few of these styles to see what they have to offer. This will help us gain a better understanding of the arts, what they are, and how they differ across the globe.

After this we will dig into the myths and philosophies that underpinned the arts for millennia. Some of which are funny, others educational, and a few (my favourites) downright ridiculous. These myths and philosophies will flesh out our grassroots understanding, allowing us to delve deeper into the stories and concepts of the arts.

Up until this time, martial arts remained isolated entities, void of international influence and only ever utilised in their home environments. But as the world opened up and international travel became easier, there was an ineluctable syncretism of cultures that led to the arts being investigated, questioned, and most importantly, tested, via outside, objective minds. This impartial analysis of the arts soon led to changes and alterations in their methods. Arts were improved, streamlined, and simplified to make them more compatible with their new international environment.

This combining and streamlining of the arts inevitably resulted in fewer available, but more efficient fighting styles. These styles have since been further questioned, broken down, and altered in the pursuit of more dynamic application. This cut-throat process has gained many advocates who relentlessly strive for the enlightenment of martial arts efficiency. The most evident culmination of this practice within a true martial arts context is the Jeet Kune Do concept. JKD, in essence, is an expression of self within a combative situation – and it is up to you to decide what that expression looks and feels like. Bruce Lee, who appeared obsessed with martial arts efficiency said we should shun 'classical mess' and aim to 'absorb what is useful, disregard what is useless and add what is specifically [our] own'. This means if something doesn't work for you, get rid of it. Don't cling onto traditions or techniques just because they work for other people. Be ruthless in your pursuit of martial arts efficiency.

Within a combative sports context, the most obvious pursuit of fighting efficiency is the global phenomenon of Mixed Martial Arts (MMA). MMA has come a long way in an incredibly short period of time. There are many reasons for this, but the pursuit of efficiency is a significant one. All you need to do to witness this progress is watch the first Ultimate Fighting Championship (UFC) competitions and compare them to what you see today. You'll see the style of fighting has changed so drastically it's almost unrecognisable. There is no longer any 'classical mess' to be found. Just tried, tested, and refined application. If we were to transport an MMA legend such as George St Pierre back in time and have him enter the first UFC, nobody would know what had hit them. He would appear as a freak of nature; a fighting machine sent back in time. His strikes more accurate than his competitor's, his transitions from standing to grappling more fluid, and his ability to strike and grapple simultaneously would dumbfound onlookers. But the techniques he would be using would not be newly developed techniques from the future. They would be the same techniques everyone else was using, just more refined, better applied, and more efficiently combined.

7

Penultimately, we will delve into the science of certain techniques to discover what the human body is capable of with good martial arts training. We will take a look at how powerfully a martial artist can punch, kick, and knee, how fast they can move, and what happens when a submission lock is applied to a joint at full force. This is an area of intense current interest as it allows us to quantify martial arts whilst sating our modern-day obsession with data.

Finally, our story will take us to the future of the arts. *What will they look like? How will they differ from what we know today? What factors will influence their development and in what ways?* Over past millennia martial arts have evolved from their initial formation to the current states we know and recognise today. *But is this their end point? Have they evolved as far as they can?* Sure, it's all speculative thinking, but it's fun, and could bear some fruit. After all, it's the ideas of today that shape the world of tomorrow.

1

THE BEGINNINGS

'Never interrupt your enemy when he is making a mistake.'

Napoleon Bonaparte

WHERE IT ALL BEGAN

When did martial arts begin? It's a good question, and I'm sorry to say I'm going to let you down before we've even started: I don't know. *Do you?* Because if you do, you should probably tell someone – maybe me so I can revise my opening to this book. The truth of the matter is nobody knows when martial arts truly began, nor do they know where they began or who started them. It's impossible to say. Posing such a question is like asking *when did the first person speak?* We could say that the first words of a certain language were spoken around a certain year, in a certain location. But we could not definitively state that the first person in the world to speak spoke *this* language and started to do so whilst inhabiting *that* location. That would be impossible to ascertain. But regardless of the point, there are a couple of things we can say about the beginnings of martial arts.

Firstly, people were obviously falling out and punching each other long before you or I turned up. The many horrific occasions of violence documented in history books tell us this. So, it seems fair to say that for as long as humans have existed, they've been falling out with each other, and fighting over territory, resources, and sexual partners. The first clear, substantial works of art depicting human combat date back to 3,400BC and are to be found in Egypt. These works of art showcase a series of positions,

9

movements, and techniques that relate to an organised fighting system that appears to represent an ancient style of Wrestling. This early style included the use of a single stick that had been specifically designed for combative purposes. We know this because the stick's construction was intentional and had been fashioned to incorporate a basket-style handguard to protect the hand of the user – a design still used today in sword-based arts like Fencing and Kenjutsu.

The Egyptians of this time also fought with clubs, shields, bows, slings, and axes. In all honesty, they sound like a pretty angry bunch. At the same time as the Egyptians were clubbing each other to death, other styles arose throughout Africa: Gidigo in Nigeria, which is an ancient form of Wrestling; Donga in Ethiopia, which incorporated the use of sticks; Musangwe in South Africa, which was a vicious form of bare-knuckle Boxing; and Engolo in Angola, which is an art heavily reliant on fast kicks and deceptive sweeps. But the forming of martial arts was not isolated to the African continent. Four hundred years later in 3,000BC, in ancient Mesopotamia, poems were scribed about battle and how the intricacies of combat are intwined throughout everyday life. These poems highlight the *art* of the martial arts and show that ever since the beginning of documented combat, art and philosophy have held a fundamental position in battle. This concept may appear incongruous at first glance, but the more it is scrutinised the more evident its truth becomes.

In Vietnam, 2,879BC, sketches and drawings were made showing moves and techniques with weapons such as swords, bows, spears, and sticks. One hundred and eighty-one years later in 2,698BC, China, the Yellow Emperor wrote detailed discourses on the martial arts alongside learnings and observations on medicine and astrology. The Yellow Emperor was also termed as being the one responsible for creating weapons, whatever that means. Another recording occurred around 2,000BC, again in Egypt, when Wrestling illustrations and detailed images of fist fighting appeared

10

on the walls of an ancient tomb belonging to Vizier Ptahhotpe of Saqqara. We can also see around the year 200BC a style known as Shǒubó, which is a no-holds-barred, hand-to-hand fighting discipline, was documented in China. This style of combat, as with all the others we have seen thus far, was another example of a calculated, considered, learned martial art.

The British, as would be expected, started Wrestling back in 1,829BC. But they didn't wrestle like everyone else (oh, no!), they tailored grappling uniforms with thick collared jackets and waistbands. This was presumably done to maximise both efficiency and style – how very British. This pattern of martial arts development and documentation emerged throughout all the world's populated areas. All of whom spent significant time devising, refining, and performing their arts. Even the Bible gets involved with a bit of scrapping when it tells how prophets and angels wrestled beasts, and how Jacob was left to wrestle inhuman creatures until the rising of the sun. Poor fella.

As for the lingering question of *who punched who first? Well, who knows?* But what we do know is that it was undeniably happening. People were hitting each other all the time, then writing poems and drawing pictures about it. People were most certainly being kicked in the groin, having their hair pulled, being poked in the eye, hit with sticks, having rocks thrown at them, being thrown on the floor, strangled, choked, dodging flying shoes, throwing ornaments, and receiving slaps across the face from their mums long into pre-history. It's in our blood; always has been and always will be. It pervades from our being and comes as naturally to humanity as procreation. Anyone with children will tell you combat is in our genes. Children will playfight continually, especially boys. They will wrestle, throw, and strike each other at any given opportunity, without any form of training or knowledge of the existence of martial arts. If the truth be told, through their inherited yearning for combat and pre-programmed defence skills, children are actually very good at fighting. Any experienced martial artist will tell you this. Unwittingly they wrestle for top position, pin their friends in established grappling holds, and use leverage to tip and trip. We are born with the instinctive nature to move, strike, and coordinate ourselves in combat. But this doesn't mean we don't have a lot to learn and that martial arts can't refine those skills as you mature. It's amazing how many adults need to be taught what children already know. I think this is because adults think too much and react too little. We tie ourselves in knots trying to calculate every eventuality, so we don't make any mistakes. The irony is this over-reliance on calculation is the biggest mistake we can make. Fights move too fast for us to contemplate our next move. We need to act in the moment and rely on our training. So, next time you're sparring or grappling in training, do yourself a favour and stop thinking too much. Be more child.

I feel this is good advice because in many ways martial arts are fun. Attend a light-hearted martial arts class or look at the faces of children as they play fight in the garden, and you will surely agree. Of course, the matter in hand is very serious: you're learning to defend yourself and your loved ones. It's a solemn business. But as with all things serious, we can't let ourselves take them too seriously. Bruce Lee even said, 'You should train seriously, but not seriously train.' And in many ways, he was right. As long as no one really gets hurt it can be fun.

Secondly, as it is with most things in the world, the beginnings of martial arts were not an isolated incident. Just like the inventions of agriculture and language, they sprang up semi-simultaneously across the globe, in complete isolation, but at roughly the same time. It's also evident, considering the anatomy of the human body is fairly uniform, that many martial arts developed similar styles and techniques completely independently of one another. Many arts learnt to throw kicks and punches in an almost identical manner even though their practitioners had never crossed paths. Others devised comparable ways of applying leverage and physics in grappling, which led to the development of similar pins and takedowns across the globe. Irrespective of how these arts manifested themselves, however, their one true commonality was that they were created with the same, singular, outcome in mind: successfully defending oneself. Imagine if next time someone threw a rock your way you had the skills, knowledge, and capability to defend yourself. Imagine if you were the Mohammed Ali of cavemen making you the first person in history who could 'float like a butterfly, sting like a bee'. This means you could dodge that flying rock (regardless of whether you deserved it or not) and escape with your face intact. Not only that, but you could successfully defend your friends, family, and other loved ones from a malicious assailant. Now, suddenly, the ability to defend yourself sounds pretty appealing.

Think about it. A country doesn't leave itself vulnerable to attack. It has a military to ensure it stays safe. There are of course countries that don't have their own militaries: Andorra, Costa Rica, the Vatican City (*who needs a military when you live with God?*) and Palau. But these countries don't sit unarmed, idly twiddling their thumbs wondering what they would do if someone invaded next Wednesday afternoon. They rely on the military forces of other countries who are contractually obliged to defend them when required. Andorra relies on Spain and France for its defences, Costa Rica and Palau are heavily dependent on the USA, and the Vatican City unofficially relies on Italy – not God.

This is an interesting way to look at defence as it's downwardly scalable to the individual. So, let's continue to shrink it down and see what we learn.

What about large businesses? Do you think they're unarmed? Unskilled in the art of defence? Of course not. Large conglomerates spend millions each year on security. They invest in cutting-edge cyber security, high-tech alarm and surveillance systems, robust properties and facilities, policies and contingency plans, and out-of-shape security guards. They outsource their defences to other companies who specialise in keeping businesses safe. *But what about small businesses?* Surely, they don't know how to defend themselves. Small businesses place shutters over windows, install visible security alarms, door locks, and digital setups. They purchase business insurance as a last line of defence should all else fail. They are as protected as they can possibly be. Even your house and possessions are protected for that matter. *Do you have a lock on your front door? What about your windows? Do you use a house alarm? Maybe you have an alarm that links directly to the police station? Fire alarm? Carbon Monoxide detector? House and contents insurance? Padlocks on your shed and a security lock on your mobile phone? Security gate? Bike lock? An unintimidating dog that pointlessly barks at passers-by?* You probably even have a lock on your toilet door to protect you from ambush whilst undertaking your business. So, now I've made my point let me ask you a question: *what about you? Do you have your own personal security skills? Can you defend yourself when needed?* We've just seen a country, conglomerate, business, house, mobile phone and shed can. *But what about you? Are you better at defending yourself than your toilet? If someone accosted you in the street and forced you to fight, could you defend yourself? Could you attack successfully or control the situation until you could escape?*

I want to ask you another question: *if not, why not? Does it not sound reasonable and responsible to have the skills to fend off an attack? To have the ability to defend your loved ones if the shit hits the fan?* There is no right or wrong answer here, just your opinion. But it's undeniably worth some thought.

Regardless of the conclusion you've drawn, many of the peoples of history thought personal defence was an important matter – as many still do today. Millions of people in different countries, from varying cultures, living amongst myriad threats, decided that defending themselves and their loved ones was of paramount importance. Important enough to dedicate significant time, thought, and resource towards. It was this decision that spurred these communities to bundle together with rigor and zest, creativity and aspiration, and aggression and calculation, in an effort to determine *what really is the best way to defend your life when all else fails?*

KUNG FU

As we have just seen, many martial arts and fighting disciplines sprouted around the world at roughly the same time. From Asia to America, and from Europe to Africa, people became obsessed with working out *what was the best way to beat each other up*? In this endeavour, as we shall discover, humanity proved surprisingly thoughtful and creative. To help us answer this question, and undoubtedly pose many more in turn, I will summarise five well-known martial arts in the hope we can all learn a little more about them. We will look at where they come from, what they are, and how they were formed and inspired. This will enable us to see a few ways in which contrasting martial arts began, how they were influenced by their immediate environments, and how people answered the looming question, *what is the best way to defend yourself?*

To begin, we'll start with a cinematic classic: Kung Fu.

When we think of Kung Fu we think of misty mountain tops, ancient temples, arduous pilgrimages, and wise old masters meditating in lotus position atop riverside rocks. *Is this far from the truth?* Well, in my experiences of Kung Fu I would say, 'yes, incredibly far from the truth – unfortunately'. But, before we get into the origins and styles of Kung Fu, let's look at how Kung Fu is classically categorised, as this will help in our understanding of the system overall.

There are two ways of breaking down Kung Fu.

Firstly, there is the separation of styles by geographical location: north and south. The northern styles of Kung Fu historically derive from a Shaolin monastery in Henan, which is the original Shaolin monastery of China. The styles that originate from

15

here are classically distinguished by their large, acrobatic movements. Within these movements it is common to find high kicks, low sweeps, flying kicks, rapid advances, circular attacks and defences, and lots of fast, powerful leg work. One of the main objectives of such styles is to inundate an opponent with a barrage of large, destructive attacks, which aim to maximise damage caused. These styles focus on deep, flexible training positions such as horse, bow, and drop stances, which aim to strengthen, stretch, and generate power in the legs. It's often said the northern styles of Kung Fu place such reliance on strong legwork because in ancient times, many people of the north rode horses (hence the existence of horse stance) which gave them strong leg muscles that they relied upon to maximise their fighting effectiveness. Examples of northern Kung Fu styles are Bajiquan, Tajiquan, Chuojiao, and the most famous of all, which graces the silver screen in almost all cinematic fighting films, Wushu. Northern styles of Kung Fu are fun to learn, artistic, and stupendous to watch when performed at a high level. I would, however, say they are notoriously difficult to master given their gymnastic requirements. The physical prowess and athleticism necessary to master Wushu are sufficient to make a grown man cry like a baby. This makes some of the northern styles less accessible than other arts, but highly rewarding if you're willing to put in the work. If you've ever seen a theatrical performance from a bald, peaceful looking, orange robed group of monks, it's highly likely the art displayed will be, or will contain, elements of Wushu. These are the styles most people think of when you mention martial arts. They are the classic, clichéd portrayal in people's minds.

On the contrary, southern styles of Kung Fu tend to be the antithesis of the north. They feature stable stances, rely little on acrobatic competency, and feature shorter, less lavish techniques such as quick, powerful punches, and short deceptive kicks. Examples of southern styles are Choy Gar, Lau Gar, Choy Li Fut, and the most famous of all southern styles, Wing Chun. Even though Wing Chun is the opposite of Wushu, it has also made a dent in cinema combat thanks to films such as *Ip Man*. I feel it would be relatively safe to say Wing Chun didn't make it into films because it looks extravagant, however. Although I can attest the art looks very good indeed when you know what you're looking at. It made its way into popular culture thanks to Bruce Lee, who was a student, advocate, and life-long practitioner of Wing Chun. Any book, film, interview, or article on Bruce Lee will tell you this. There is also proof of Wing Chun's influence in his martial arts legacy, as Wing Chun's impact is to be found in Bruce Lee's own style of Kung Fu, Jun Fan Gung Fu, which he formed in 1960.

The second classical way of breaking down Kung Fu is by style: internal and external. This form of classification is somewhat flawed in my opinion, as any experienced martial artist will tell you that all traditional martial arts contain both internal and external elements so are wholly exclusive to neither. We saw this at the beginning of the book when we learned that people were fighting with clubs and axes then writing poems about it. We can also see the presence of both within a typical martial arts class. For instance, hitting pads, sparring, and practicing lock and release flows on a live opponent are *external*, whilst focusing on breathing as we strike and move, and drilling techniques and movements until they are a subconscious reflex are *internal*.

The classically perceived *external* arts are typified by their fast, aggressive, explosive movements. These arts place a significant focus on agility, flexibility, and strength. As you can see, the labelling *external* in this case is entirely apt, and examples of such arts are Wushu and Nam Pai Chuan.

As for the classically perceived *internal* styles of Kung Fu, these arts focus predominantly on the interconnecting of mind, body, and spirit. They introduce and focus heavily on the notion of *Chi*, which is the supposed breath and energy that flows throughout the body. The aim of this focusing is to harness the energy of Chi, which is believed to make you more powerful and less prone to injury. As far as I'm aware the existence of Chi has never been robustly proven, and by simply mentioning it you can cause ruptures of laughter from martial artists of more modern styles. But many traditional martial artists confidently assert its existence. The concept of Chi is not exclusive to the Chinese arts, however, and can be found throughout other countries too. Within an *internal* style, offensive and defensive focus is fixated more on relaxation and leverage than outright strength and aggression. Examples of such arts are Xing Yi Quan and the most famous of all, Tai Chi.

If we break away from our conversation on Kung Fu classifications, we can use our time to look at a few different styles. A lot of styles of Kung Fu have their roots and beginnings in the teachings of Buddhism, which made its way to China from India. It's told in legend that the holy Buddhist figures who pilgrimaged to China brought with them 18 positions, known as 18 hands, which were soon converted into 18 martial postures before being combined, for the sake of practice and repetition, into a martial form – a series of movements, like a dance. These 18 postures were then doubled to 36 before being increased again to 173. Then, roughly 200 years later, the 18 original hands were completed in 18 forms, with each form having 18 postures, making 324 postures in all. Today, these postures are considered to have been the beginnings of Kung Fu.

Once this base of 324 postures had been established, the Chinese people started to get creative with their fighting methods and looked to their direct environment for inspiration. As it is often said, 'you find inspiration in the most unusual of places'; in this instance, this proved to be entirely correct. Many Kung Fu enthusiasts took inspiration from the animals that surrounded them. The early Kung Fu fighters watched the animals of China and analysed how they behaved in combat. They then mimicked those movements before incorporating them into their fighting repertoire. This was done because it was believed that by mimicking an animal the practitioner would inherit its qualities. If this is true, then I think you can tell a lot about a person by the type of animal they impersonate. Especially the guy in the corner pretending to be a penguin. Many styles were conceived using this method, but the five main animal styles created were: tiger, leopard, crane, snake, and dragon – I'm not sure who claimed they'd seen a dragon in a fight. Even though the five main animal styles originated in the north, their movements and influence are greater associated with southern Kung Fu styles as their techniques tend to be sharp, short, and direct – at least in most instances.

Naming a fighting style after a tiger does seem quite cool, but once people caught wind of what was happening the naming of styles after animals went viral. Suddenly, numerous animal substyles began to appear, such as monkey, panther, boar, eagle, praying mantis, hawk, falcon, heron, phoenix (not even a real animal), wolf, and lion. But as with all things, some people always take it too far: Imperial Cobra Kung Fu, Spider Kung Fu, Tibetan Ghost Bat Kung Fu(!), Rhino Kung Fu, Chicken Kung Fu, Crab Kung Fu (treatable with cream) Manta Ray Kung Fu, Duck Kung Fu (absolutely quackers), Elephant Kung Fu, Frog & Toad Kung Fu (named after the local pub) and Dog Kung Fu. And just in case you were wondering, tell-tale Dog Kung Fu attacks are eye gouging, throat attacks, finger breaking, leg breaks, and even tearing off lips and ears. So, next time a toy poodle is gazing at you from across the room, don't say I didn't warn you.

KARATE

Gentleman first, warrior second. That is the way of Karate.

Karate is a stand-up striking Okinawan martial art that originated on the beautiful, sand-fringed islands of the Okinawan prefecture, which is a cluster of roughly 150 islands sat in the East China Sea. The art focuses predominantly on striking with the hands, elbows, knees, and feet, with some styles incorporating ground fighting and joint-locking techniques. The deep roots of

Karate are not exclusively Okinawan, however. Just as Kung Fu was born from a series of Indian meditation movements, Karate was born from a significant Chinese Kung Fu influence, chiefly the southern art of Fujian White Crane. The difference is that although we can see Kung Fu originated from 18 meditative positions that were introduced to the country by Buddhists, there is no agreed upon consensus as to exactly how the Chinese martial arts influenced the formation of Karate. Some say elements of the Chinese arts were brought to Okinawa on pilgrimages, as the wandering Chinese nomads set sail in pursuit of better lives in mysterious foreign lands. Others believe merchants and tradespeople carried Kung Fu movements to the Okinawan archipelago whilst visiting the islands in search of profits. There are numerous theories to be found about how the foundations of Karate were formed, many of which orientate around similar stories and themes. But even though the exact means of influence are not agreed upon, it can be seen from the perspective of the trained eye that there is most certainly a Chinese influence when it comes to the basal movements of the three original Okinawan Karate fighting systems: Shuri-te, Naha-te and Tomari-te. Each of which was devised by an individual family. All of which are named after the cities from which they emerged.

In 1609 the samurai Shimazu clan invaded Okinawa in a brutal and bloody attempt to claim the idyllic subtropical islands as their own. Fully clad in samurai attire, the Shimazu clan fought sword in hand until a state of despot rule was established over the prefecture. Hitherto, the art of Karate had blossomed throughout the islands and equipped kings, merchants, and peasants alike with the skills required to defend themselves. Skills, which in this instance, proved inadequate against the samurai's refined and tenacious Bushido. But after the islands' reluctant submission, the pursuit of martial arts was prohibited, the wielding of weapons banned, and the people of the region physically and emotionally suppressed. This incursion and its totalitarian repercussions forced Karate into the undergrowth compelling it to become a secretive, hidden, empty-

20

handed art. Nevertheless, the people of the Okinawa region proved themselves to be a hardy, disobedient bunch, even in the face of mortal danger, as it didn't take long before the empty-handed art was armed once more and ready to be practiced again. The difference was that this time, the weapons in use were not the swords and knives of time passed, but old, rusty, tetanus inducing farming tools from the workers' fields. These labouring tools allowed the practitioners to study both empty-handed and armed techniques in the fields without raising the suspicion of the samurai. Curiously, history appears to show that regardless of their iron-fisted subjugation, the samurai never once became suspicious of numerous Japanese men stood in fields beating the hell out of each other with tonfas, sais, and sticks. This enforced outcome is why many styles of Karate, including those in the west, use Far Eastern agricultural tools as weapons instead of the traditional swords and shields that many of the other arts of this period employ. Nonetheless, by this point, Karate had developed into a strong, dangerous, and effective fighting system with solid roots that had taken an unshakeable hold in Okinawan society. And regardless of their desires and intent, it proved too late for the samurai to distinguish the art.

After hundreds of years of suppressed Karate practice under the dictatorial rule of the samurai, the Okinawa archipelago was annexed in 1879. At the turn of the 20th century, permission was given to end the shroud of secrecy that had surrounded the art for 270 years. From this moment forth, Karate exploded into the mainstream, opening its ways to the general population and the mainland of Japan. Karate and its enticing philosophies quickly infiltrated Japanese culture, and before long, they had seeped into the education system and soon formed part of the Japanese curriculum. But the Japanese were not the only ones smitten with the art. Many US servicepeople posted on the islands during World War II also became advocates of its ways. It's a charming thought that regardless of the USA and Japan's strained relationship during the war, many US personnel ended up studying the ways of Karate under Japanese masters before eventually taking its methods and values back home. This is the reason why an established Karate culture exists in the US today. It was born of the most unprecedented relationship between two enemies who took different sides in the biggest war in human history. Proof that peace and understanding can be found amid madness.

The pursuit of Karate is a strict path to walk. Unlike the Chinese arts that tend to be less hierarchical, the Japanese arts have a propensity to be harsher, more respectful, and greater in their forms of discipline. This makes Karate a great choice of art for disruptive children, or those lacking structure and discipline in life. The rigours, learnings, and comradery of Karate are a tried and tested method for building strength, fitness, confidence, and character. As well as everything else it has to offer, Karate also ingrains a stout focus on courtesy, respect, humility, and non-violence within its students, known as *kokoro*. This strict form of tutelage is heavily derived from the substantial respect and obedience that is to be found within Japanese society. Let me tell you here that you would not dare question an old-school Karate master. You would accept their learnings as gospel and do exactly what you were told. Questioning their theories, techniques, and methods would be akin to blasphemy. If somehow you did summon the courage to seriously question an old master's techniques, you would find out the hard way that they were extremely effective. This form of strict discipline has its obvious advantages, as it produce respectful, dedicated, robust martial artists. But the drawbacks of such teaching methods are also evident as they could result in the eventual stagnation of the system through lack of objectiv questioning and analysis. But the aim of all this discipline is not to squash a student's freedom of expression – Karate is not dictatorship by any means. The aim is to embrace maximum respec for your instructor, contemporaries, opponents, and mo importantly, self. It's a means of nurturing universal respect amor all.

As an art, Karate is a self-defence method through and through. Unlike other arts, such as some of the Shaolin arts we explored above, Karate was formed based on self-protection. It was not created from positions and techniques taken from other philosophies and practices, which were then adapted and transformed into fighting techniques. The first movement in Karate was decisively made with the intent to defend oneself, and I believe it would be safe to say that every movement thrown in a Karate session since has been undertaken with the same intent. Primarily, the aim for a new Karate student is to overcome and overpower their opponent. Katas are performed and techniques drilled until the student develops the required physical attributes to win. Once the student reaches a high-level within the art, the focus shifts from defeating opponents to overcoming the limitations of oneself. The same methods are utilised in this battle of self (courage, discipline, commitment, respect), with the only difference being that the student must now look inside to their own demons in the pursuit of internal development. Karate is a hard, physical martial art, and due to this physical robustness, it is normally intertwined with spells of kneeling meditation both before and after practice. Students are often encouraged to undertake meditation in their own time outside of class to help with overall development and to ensure their thoughts, ways, and movements do not become too *hard*. In the true essence of Karate, and to achieve the zenith of your potential, the primary focus should be towards maturity, self-understanding, finesse, enlightenment, and inner peace. Karate encourages students to practice each move to such an extent that thought dissolves and only flowing emptiness remains. Movements are no longer needed to be considered, processed, and thought about. The body simply moves all on its own. In the words of Gichin Funakoshi, the late founder of Shotokan Karate-Do: 'Form is emptiness, emptiness is form itself.'

WRESTLING

The oldest martial art, without question, is Wrestling. If you were accosted during an outing tomorrow, the resulting scuffle would almost certainly end up a Wrestling match. We can also confidently state that if 5,000 years ago a humble hunter-gatherer ended up in a fight, it too would have become a Wrestling bout. It is one of, if not the most primal of activities. An activity that is hardcoded into our genes and has been for millennia. The Greeks, Romans, Nigerians, Indians, Chinese, Japanese, English, Spanish, Mongolians, Russians, Angolans, French, and Romanians did it – and still do. Without any form of training, even children do it. If you have children, next time they playfight, pay attention to how they move, push, counter and pin each other. If you've never done this before, I'm sure you'll be surprised by the quality of technique you see. Wrestling is our forte, and always has been. It is up there with the most primal of human instincts, which is why we're so good at it.

But let's not flatter ourselves too early on as Wrestling is not exclusively a human endeavour. Apes have been witnessed wrestling on multiple occasions. Just take a trip to the zoo and you'll likely see it for yourself. For the record, bears, tigers, house cats, dogs, squirrels, mice, and racoons have also been seen wrestling each other. Most animals have some form of Wrestling instinct in their genes, which is why I am presuming you don't find any of this surprising. It feels rather natural to imagine animals of varying species wrestling each other. *But what would your response be if I said bears, tigers, house cats, dogs, squirrels, and racoons know Karate? Or that all these animals are competent in Kendo?* That, obviously, would be preposterous, and your reaction would most certainly be equal in measure. This reaction illustrates just how innate Wrestling is across multiple species and how primitive and instinctive it is as a means of fighting.

This ingrained aptitude for Wrestling lies at the core of the art's beauty. But don't be fooled by its familiarity. Wrestling is one of, if not the most difficult of martial arts. It's an art that grinds the body down into a pool of exhaustion. It's a skill that requires flexibility, strength, speed, suppleness, timing, coordination, intelligence, deceit, and aggression to master. A high-level wrestler is one of the world's finest martial artists, making Wrestling one of the world's most effective martial arts.

From an anthropological perspective, the beginnings of Wrestling are murky and fragmented. Wrestling, as a sport, has existed for as long as we have – probably longer if our observations of other species are anything to go by. The proof of which can be found in paintings, poems, and cave markings throughout the world. It appears that humans, especially males, have been borderline obsessed with Wrestling since antiquity. People have been throwing each other around for a really long time, and as a species, we've become pretty damn good at it.

One of the oldest depictions of Wrestling yet discovered is a carved stone slab showing three pairs of semi-naked wrestlers locked in combat around 3,000BC. Further markings of Wrestling's early saturation of society have also been found across the globe. From a beautiful bronze figurine in Iraq, 2,600BC; numerous Egyptian tomb paintings, circa 2,400BC; and textual descriptions of fierce Greek Wrestling bouts that occurred during the Olympic Games, Olympia, Greece, 704BC. There are ample ancient references to Wrestling to be unveiled. Even the great Greek philosopher, Plato, was known to dabble in the art. One of the most splendid observations from all these markings is that the belts worn on the Iraqi figurine and the techniques shown in the Egyptian tomb paintings are still in use today. Five thousand years later, almost everything seen in ancient Wrestling styles is still being trained, taught, and refined in local clubs and arenas. What an astounding thought! This continued practice of antique techniques and drills raises another point worth serious consideration: the Wrestling of old has proven itself so instinctive, efficient, and effective, that 5,000 years of rehearsal, analysis, technological innovation, and influence have barely changed its ways. Try to think of any cultural or human practice 5,000 years old that has barely changed. *Pottery?* Technology has changed pottery techniques substantially. *Agriculture?* Evidently agricultural techniques have vastly improved. *What about building?* Building techniques have clearly improved, otherwise you'd be reading this book in an adobe hut. So, if you want a real taste of human history, to feel your primordial instincts flare and connect with the cultures and people of old, my advice would be to wrestle. It's the closest you'll ever come to time travel.

In modern society, Wrestling is classically broken down into three types: Belt-and-Jacket, Catch-Hold, and Loose. Belt-and-Jacket Wrestling is exactly as it sounds. Wrestlers wear clothing that can be used as a means of leverage by their opponent. This style of Wrestling allows for additional techniques, holds, and locks, whilst proving to be a sport that has a realistic transition potential to a self-defence art. *When was the last time you left the house naked?* Given it was likely a long time ago, if ever, it would be safe to say that when you leave the house you probably wear some form of jacket, jumper, trousers, or belt, etc. These items of clothing are essentially the Belt-and-Jacket of Wrestling, meaning all techniques practiced in this type can be applied to individuals walking the street. Unless you live in a nudist colony of course, in which case they'll just have to grab a hold of something else. Examples of this type of Wrestling are Cornish (UK), Gouren (Brittany), Khuresh (Siberia), and Shuai Jiao (China). The most well-known of this type today are Judo and Sambo.

The second type of Wrestling, Catch-Hold, requires contestants to establish a set hold before combat begins. In most instances this hold must be maintained throughout the fight as the opponents battle to stay on their feet. If the hold is broken, the opponents must reset their position and start over. This type of Wrestling was created in Great Britain, circa 1870, and is most famous for its use of holds, locks, and submissions to maximise its effectiveness. Its techniques and practices have proven so effective they are prevalent in modern day MMA, as well as being showily incorporated into the superfluous performances of Show Wrestling. Due to its origins and recent emergence, most styles of Catch Wrestling are to be found in and around the UK. Separate regions of the UK developed their own styles of Catch Wrestling from Cumberland, Devon, and Lancashire. Its influence is also to be found in India and Ireland, for reasons relating to the UK's relationship with these two countries in the recent past.

Lastly, Loose Wrestling begins with the opponents completely separated. From their detached position the wrestlers must fight to establish any grip they desire (within reason) and force their opponent to the ground. The fluid, fast, and unpredictable nature of this type of Wrestling makes it appealing to many, which is why it is often found in modern international competitions. One such example of Loose Wrestling is the well-known Greco-Roman, which is famous for its explosive nature and spectacular throws and takedowns.

As it is with a lot of martial arts, by looking at the movements, methods, and techniques used, it is possible to learn about the people who created and refined the art in its early days. From this point, we are able to draw some form of understanding of the art's environment, the people who called it home, and the skills required to survive in that space. There really is a lot to be learnt by simply looking at a martial art. To exemplify this point, let's look at a few Wrestling arts and their sometimes-humorous idiosyncrasies.

Lancashire Wrestling (UK): A historic style known for its aggressive methods and no-holds-barred techniques.

Devonshire Wrestling (UK): A Belt-and-Jacket style that allows throws and takedowns but no ground fighting. Competitors of this style wore wooden clogs and could kick their opponents to inflict injury. This style is now believed to be extinct.

Glima (Iceland): Glima is the national sport of Iceland, which traces its lineage back to the times of the Vikings. In this style, wrestlers sometimes wear leather harnesses around the thighs and waist that can be used to hold, pin, and throw opponents.

Trântă (Romania): This style, found in both Romania and Moldova, is an upright art where the opponents fight to win a loaf of bread.

Sumo (Japan): One of the most famous styles of Wrestling where two very large opponents fight inside a ring on the ground. The aim is to make the opponent touch the ground or force them out of the ring with anything except the soles of the feet. Wrestlers are even allowed to slap and strike their opponent with an open palm.

Gidigbo (Nigeria): An extremely traditional form of Wrestling that is augmented by mysticism, spirits, and religion. The wrestlers' religious powers are summoned as a means of influence and defence to help them attain victory.

Oil Wrestling (Western Asia): The practitioners of this style do exactly what you'd imagine. They don leather trousers, oil themselves up, and go for it.

NINJUTSU

Everybody has heard of the ninja, which is rather ironic. But this widespread knowledge of a creed of skilled combatants is a modern day affair. The ninja of years passed were not know to the masses as they are today. Their identities remained out of sight and out of mind as they lurked in the shadows on the peripherals of society. They were a band of veiled warriors trained in myriad disciplines who, if folklore is to be believed, descended from a demon who was half man, half three-legged crow.

The name, Ninjutsu, can be broken down into two parts. The first of which is the character 'Nin', which means to apply one's heart, thoughts, and ego to the edge of the sword. This character places focus on a would-be combatant's commitment to the way of the ninja, by ensuring every action, decision and thought a person made was fully weighted, calculated, and committed to the cause. It also placed significant focus on the eradication of ego, which held no place in the study of Ninjutsu. The second part of the name, 'Jutsu', essentially means 'technique'. As most martial arts do, Ninjutsu presented itself as an expression of self through the refinement of martial technique. This combination of correct focus, commitment, absence of ego, and perfect technique, was the essence of Ninjutsu. It was simply not possible to become a ninja without it.

The original art of Ninjutsu was believed to have been formed by a rogue band of samurai from the Nanboku-cho period (1336-1392). As you would imagine, high-quality sources confirming this story are hard to come by due to the secrecy that surrounded Ninjutsu in its earliest years. If a samurai was defeated in battle, they were obligated to commit ritualistic suicide known as *seppuku* or *hara-kiri*. This is because in samurai culture, failure in any form was not tolerated, and any samurai who did happen to fail was ordered to death. It's no surprise then that upon defeat in battle these corrupt samurai opted to flee society as opposed to choosing the path of self-disembowelment. In their efforts to escape death, the group fled to the quieter more rural regions of society in the hope they would not be recognised and extradited. It was during these times whilst hiding from the powers that be that the fleeing samurai noticed a rather insidious opportunity. A gap in the market as we would call it today. Their ploy was to operate in the cracks and shadows as a band of highly trained martial artists, who would place themselves on the market as assassins, spies, and scouts for hire. The main driver for this anti-authority rebellion was that many of the everyday Japanese people felt culturally opposed to the ruling samurai class. These disenfranchised populations loathed the samurai. They wanted them gone; and this rogue band of samurais appeared to agree. They too wanted to disrupt society and witness an end to the samurai's despotic rule. Japan was trapped in a state of political turmoil, and the frustration, anger, and uncertainty this created amongst the population left ample space within society for Ninjutsu. It didn't take long before their skills, knowledge, and inimical ways were in demand. The ninja's methods proved popular, and many territorial lords and corrupt samurai were soon sourcing the ninja's skills to stifle, manipulate, and overthrow the iron-fist of authority.

Contrary to popular belief, however, which has been formed and tainted by present day entertainment, the ninja's core function was not assassination but espionage. Nor were they turtles. Amassing and reporting back information was their primary objective, which given the demanding prerequisites of their discipline, they performed with the utmost expertise. As was dictated by the ambitious requirements of their existence, the pursuit of Ninjutsu and the mastering of its skills proved to be an endeavour not suited to the fainthearted. Training to be a ninja was an arduous, dangerous, and taxing affair. To give their ordeal a more familiar context, the mastering of Ninjutsu in ancient Japan would likely be comparable to joining the Special Forces today. Only the grittiest individuals who proved to be both mentally and physically robust were suited to the task. And in order to become a fully-fledged ninja in the 1500s, all budding recruits were expected to master 18 unique disciplines.

1. **Seishin Teki Kyoyo (Spiritual Refinement)**: The first stage of Ninjutsu development entails detailed introspection to clarify an individual's strengths, weaknesses, and the influence they have over their own existence and outcomes. Before any martial training begins, an individual must be clear on their intentions and commitments, and they must understand their motivations in life. Ninjutsu is an ardent advocate of knowing oneself before

the pursuit of personal development begins, meaning this stage consisted of seven focal areas: self-knowing, knowledge of nature, the calling (understanding destiny), harmony (being still like water), the heart (to understand and have empathy), the eye (to see clearly), and love (love for oneself and others). Only once these areas had been fully understood could a ninja continue on their path to enlightenment.

2. **Tai Jutsu (Unarmed Combat)**: In order to master the requirement of unarmed combat, students refined their skills within several areas: Daken-Taijutsu (striking, blocking, and kicking); Jutai-Jutsu (grappling, choking, and escaping the holds of others); and Taihenjutsu (silent movement, leaping, tumbling, and rolling). Each of which were considered integral to a rounded, unarmed ninja.

3. **Ninja Ken (Ninja Sword)**: Stage three focused on the use of a short, straight, single edged blade, which was the ninja's primary weapon of choice. When training with this weapon the ninja fixated on two main methods of use: the *fast draw*, which involved drawing and cutting with the blade in a sharp, simultaneous movement, and *fencing skills*, which were to be used if a ninja was forced into a face-to-face confrontation.

4. **Bo-Jutsu (Stick and Staff Fighting)**: The Ninja trained with a variety of sticks, especially those used by the samurai at the time. The reason for this intense focus on the samurai's weapons was because it was a ubiquitous belief amongst the ninja that mastering your enemy's weapons was as important as mastering your own. The ninja also created and practiced with specially designed Shinobi-Zue, or Ninja Canes, which were deceptive sticks that contained secret blades, chains, and poisoned darts.

5. **Shuriken-Jutsu (Throwing Blades)**: Throwing knives and blades were carried on the person and were used as a means of initiating (or ending) combat from a distance. The most famous of which is a four-pointed throwing star named, Senban Shuriken.

6. **Yari-Jutsu (Spear Fighting)**: Spears were used to cover middle-range combat. By this stage of the process, it is clear to see the ninja were becoming proficient in multi-range combative systems and were now able to attack and defend themselves from varying distances. The main spears studied at this stage of development were the short spear, long spear, metal spear, three bladed spear, and halfmoon bladed spear. Each of which served its own deadly purpose.

7. **Naginata-Jutsu (Halberd Fighting)**: A short blade mounted onto a long handle that was used for slashing enemies at a medium range.

8. **Kusari-Gama (Chain and Sickle):** This medieval looking weapon consisted of a six to nine-foot chain with a weighted object attached to one end and a razor-sharp sickle on the other. The weighted object was used to strike the opponent from a distance after being swung by the chain in a circular motion to generate momentum. The resulting impact of such a strike was entirely sufficient to kill or maim an enemy. The chain section of the weapon was used to entangle and ensnare an opponent, making them easier to attack and kill. The sickle was reserved for stabbing and hacking if an opponent encroached too closely. It's a truly horrific weapon.

9. **Kayaku-Jutsu (Fire and Explosives)**: The use and manufacturing of bombs and timed explosives.

10. **Henso-Jutsu (Disguise and Impersonation)**: Being a successful ninja means sneaking through defences, extracting highly sensitive information, falsifying identities, and impersonating people of influence. To achieve these skills the ninja learnt to mimic personality traits, body language, and speech. Their studies in this area focused on learning the *seven ways of going*, which orientated around the ability to successfully impersonate seven important individuals: a monk, samurai, merchant, craftsman, farmer, performer, and an ordinary person. Although the necessity for this stage is evident, its presence feels somewhat like a theatre school intervention amid Special Forces training.

11. **Shinobi-Iri (Stealth and Entering Methods)**: This is probably the most famed of ninja skillsets and what most people think of when they think of Ninjutsu. Breaking and entering were staple skills of the ninja. As was moving silently, staying in the shadows, and covering large distances unnoticed. This is the stage that enabled practitioners to disappear into the darkness and remain there indefinitely. To do this the ninja focused on five principal areas: correct timing, analysis of defence and weak point recognition, weakness in staff/guard locations, the use of objects for distraction purposes, and the art of concealing sound. By applying the correct combination of skills to a given situation it was believed no location was impenetrable.

12. **Ba-Jutsu (Horsemanship):** Ninja were taught to be proficient on horseback, both in riding and mounted combat skills. But riding and fighting from horseback was not the only focus of this faze. Ninja also learnt to care for their horse, and the horse was further trained how to manage its reactions in testing situations. It appears even ninja horses attended theatre school.

13. **Sui-Ren (Water Training)**: So that trainees were able to operate efficiently in all environments, a large focus was placed on stealth swimming, silent movement through water, the use of boats and floats, and underwater combat techniques.

14. **Bo-Ryaku (Strategy)**: This stage of a ninja's development fixated on political plots, battle tactics, deception, and the use of advantageous timing within current affairs. Sort of like an olden day Cambridge Analytica. A major point of focus was the ability to influence outside forces that would overspill and result in beneficial changes to inside situations. This stage of Ninjutsu development was essentially the dissecting of mass manipulation. The art of flicking an upright domino and watching the rest tumble in turn.

15. **Cho Ho (Espionage)**: Espionage was the rock-solid foundation of age-old Ninjutsu. Espionage training focused chiefly on manipulating and recruiting outsiders, building trust, surveillance techniques and methods, and environmental analysis. Each of the 18 disciplines we are working through were of great importance to Ninjutsu, but tried, tested, razor-sharp espionage skills were considered the icing on the deceptive cake.

16. **Inton-Jutsu (Escape and Concealment)**: As you can imagine honing the ability to invade and extract information from sensitive environments is one thing. *But what happens if you're there, the shit hits the fan, and you need a quick way out?* This is what the ninja rehearsed during escape and concealment training: the ability to disappear and slip out unnoticed. To achieve this the Goton-Po five elements (earth, water, fire, metal, and wood) were studied so they could be utilised during escapes.

17. **Ten-Mon (Meteorology)**: Meteorological education was relied upon so the ninja could use the weather and its seasonal nuances to their advantage. Techniques such as staying downwind from your enemies, moving with, as opposed to into the rain, and forecasting future conditions to assist with reconnaissance and intelligence missions were on the list.

18. **Chi-Mon (Geography)**: Lastly, Ninjutsu focused on the study of geography and topography, allowing the ninja to creep throughout their environment without getting caught. This knowledge also assisted with evasion, breaking and entering, and rapid escape techniques.

Ninjutsu focussed heavily on producing incredibly well-rounded combatants, capable of much more than simply defending themselves. The true aim of Ninjutsu was not just the refinement of martial art. Its objective was outright subterfuge. Insidious warfare by any means necessary. The reason for this is because the beginnings of Ninjutsu differ from the other arts we have seen so far. Kung Fu, Karate, and Wrestling were all arts most likely developed outside combative situations, which could be refined over time and used in combat when it reared its ugly head. Ninjutsu on the other hand is a martial art devised amid combat. An art focussed entirely on military application. This is what made Ninjutsu different from many other arts. This is why Ninjutsu evolved not just as a series of self-defence techniques, but as a vicious, dirty, gritty, bloody, deceptive means of combat.

CAPOEIRA

Have you ever wanted to learn to fight whilst looking seriously cool in the process? Then it's time you learned about Capoeira.

Capoeira is often labelled as a 'martial art infused dance', or as Mestre Jelon Vieira describes it, 'a dance which is a fight, and a fight which is a dance'. It looks so good that its presence is visible within other disciplines such as street acrobatics, break dancing, and parkour. It would be unwise, however, to dismiss Capoeira based on its looks, because its unorthodox methods, techniques, and movements, which make it so appealing in the first place, are also the basis for its deceptive functionality. The reason for this is because Capoeira's lavish movements form a self-fulfilling cycle: its movement becomes lost in movement. And this movement has a name: *ginga*, or more commonly, the *rocking step*. This, as you would imagine, makes Capoeira incredibly difficult to predict. If you've ever practiced martial arts, you'll know it's sometimes problematic enough countering a kick from a stationary position. Chuck in a bunch of additional movement before the kick is even thrown and you can imagine how difficult things can get. But, as with some of the arts we have seen so far, Capoeira's efficiency is often called into question, which is by no means surprising, nor a bad thing. The questioning of efficiency and realism in martial arts is a forever cycling conversation. Even the arts that have proven themselves under pressure time and time again don't escape this relentless scrutiny. Therefore, Capoeira's inclusion in this opening list is not without controversy, as depending on who you ask you will be told Capoeira is either a dance, game, or as is purported in this book, a martial art. But there isn't really a correct answer here, only differing interpretations.

The origins of Capoeira are murky, as is the way with a lot of old martial arts. Many scholars, historians, Capoeiristas, and anthropologists believe Capoeira's foundations were laid in the 16th century by bands of slaves taken from western Africa to Brazil by the Portuguese. Once in Brazil, the lives of the Africans were forcibly changed due to the unfamiliar nature of their new environment, and the outright suppression suffered at the hands of their abductors. The powers of the time prohibited the practicing of martial arts and forcibly stifled any form of cultural expression. The Africans, however, proved stubborn in their resolve, and in the face of racist suppression, Capoeira was born. The immediate question arising from this situation is *how did droves of African slaves form and refine a martial art directly under the noses of their self-interested masters without raising suspicion?* The answer, in true African style, is they disguised Capoeira as a dance. Even today, due to the art's birth amidst such barbaric suppression, Capoeira is not just considered a form of self-defence, but a survival tool and means of cultural identity. The art has even been granted a special protected status as a form of intangible cultural heritage by UNESCO.

When practiced in a mock combative setting (or playing the game as it's known) Capoeira practitioners fight to a rhythmic beat played upon a Ngoma drum, a Berimbau (a single-stringed musical bow), a Pandeiro (a hand frame drum), an Agogô (a bell), a Conga (a tall, narrow, single-headed drum), and the superb sounding Reco-reco (a scraping percussion instrument). The harmony created by these instruments forms the symbolic sound of Capoeira culture. The most important of the listed instruments is the Berimbau, as the lead Berimbau player commands the authority to dictate who moves next and at what speed they move. The Berimbau player can also slow the rhythm to calm the fighters down if things get too rough, or if needed, stop the game entirely. This way of training will appear unusual to martial artists of other styles, because the thought of sparring to a beat, which dictates the speed and aggression of the fight will feel absurd. But many things in martial arts appear absurd to the outside eye. Only using your hands (Boxing) will appear strange to some; placing an overriding emphasis on fighting on the ground (some forms of Jiu Jitsu) can also seem bizarre; *what about learning to wield antiquated weapons*? (Karate); *or mainly learning to fight from kicking range?* (Taekwondo). These methods will appear counterproductive to some. So, training to a rhythm dictated by a drummer is just another means of artistic expression, which is neither right nor wrong, just different. And no one who trains in

37

martial arts will be able to deny that solid rhythm and timing (and the ability to break them) are effective weapons.

The barbarous clampdown on African culture by the Portuguese had the predictable side-effect: small groups of slaves rebelled against the authoritarian rule. The Africans proved that not only could they dance, fight, and bring light to the darkest of situations; they showed that with a smile on their face and rhythm in their step they could betray the Portuguese by forming small, counter-cultural bands known as *Quilombos*. These groups consisted of rebellious Brazilian natives, escaped slaves, and Europeans fleeing Christian extremism. As this motley community gained momentum, more and more people became convinced by its methods and ideologies, which led to larger numbers of individuals migrating inwards. Due to this influx of ideological adoption, it didn't take long for the Quilombos to establish a strong foothold within society. A foothold that would eventually lead to the development of a rough, independent, multi-ethnic state that shunned Portuguese rule, formed its own cultures and traditions, and revived the suppressed cultural norms of their homelands. As the existence of the Quilombos became known, the powers that be predictably attempted to extinguish them. It was at this point that Capoeira made its most dramatic transition from a culturally expressive tool to an outright martial art that proved so effective in its environment, the governor announced Capoeira was 'harder to defeat…than the Dutch invaders'.

The perennial resilience of the slaves and their Capoeira eventually grew so strong that larger and larger movements were established. The threat of prison, punishment, and publicly displayed execution did not prove to be sufficient threats to stop the rebellious slaves and the use of Capoeira. It also wasn't long before the slaves' movement gained momentum on the political front, which proved to be the kindling that led to the abolition of slavery. The fire of freedom burnt fiercely within the slaves, and eventually, on 13 May 1888, the *Golden Law* was passed and slavery in Brazil rightfully disappeared into the history books.

The passing of the Golden Law did not prove to be the panacea it was anticipated to be, however. As when slavery was abolished, a lack of foresight from the political powers of the time meant no security net was established for the 'fallout' that the ending of slavery would cause. This meant as soon as the Golden Law was passed, many Africans lost their jobs, homes, and livelihoods with nowhere to turn, and no social security to assist. This political ineptness predictably forced the now free Africans into a life of crime, which remained the only route available to provide for themselves and their families. It would be fair to state by this time that many Africans had developed a justified hate for Brazil, which I am sure eased the burden of criminality. *But how would the Africans survive in their criminal environment*? They would employ the tried, tested, and refined ways of Capoeira. Capoeira practitioners were hired as bodyguards and hitmen, whose skills would be used to seek revenge, make profit, and influence political decisions through intimidation and assassination. Brazil went into freefall as hordes of angry, armed minorities waged war on its towns and cities. Africans, native blacks, mixed race individuals, poverty-stricken whites, and Portuguese immigrants all joined the movement in revolt against the ruling bourgeois.

Capoeira's struggles did not end here, however, as in the 1890s it was outlawed, and anyone found practicing Capoeira was punished. These punishments ranged from death to a severe beating and the severing of the Achilles tendon. As would be expected, the threat of such punishment made practitioners cautious. As a means of self-protection, the Capoeiristas created a special drum rhythm called, *cavalaria,* which signified the presence of police within the area. Upon hearing this distinctive rhythm, Capoeiristas would flee into the alleys and backstreets. Capoeira students also gave each other nicknames to conceal their true identities. A tradition that still exists today within many schools and academies.

This outlawing of Capoeira almost drove the art to extinction. Its illegality and the threat of severe punishment forced thousands of Capoeiristas to ditch their beloved art if they wished to live any semblance of a normal life. But, on the brink of dissolution, in the city of Salvador, one man named Manuel dos Reis Machado refused to let go. He held tightly to the art in an act of defiance that saved Capoeira from extinction. It's thanks to him we can enjoy the beauty of Capoeira today. That we can feel its rhythm, marvel at its beauty, and learn to dance in the darkest of moments.

DIVERSITY IN MARTIAL ARTS

There are thousands of martial arts in the world, of which we have briefly encountered five. It is evident that all five of these arts have profoundly different beginnings, methods, techniques, stories, histories, theories, inspirations, and applications. This is exactly why I chose these five arts. I wanted to show how contrasting martial arts can be, and how their environments, people, and situations made them what they are. I also chose these five arts because they represent a good spread across the globe, from Asia and Europe to Africa and the Americas. They are a good sample to demonstrate diversity in martial arts in their earlier days.

These five arts are also some of the most widespread, well-known martial arts in the world. Almost everyone has heard of a few of them, if not all. They represent some of the biggest historical archives in martial arts. They are duly recognised by modern society and their ways have been practiced, questioned, and embraced by millions worldwide. They also present five distinct ways of answering the question: *what is the best way to defend yourself?* Evidently, each art's answering of the question differed because they were all born into unique circumstances. Developing a martial art from scratch during a period when martial arts were illegal, and the population enslaved, will most certainly produce a different result from a martial art devised in an open, accepting society during peacetime. It's also interesting to note that even though each of these arts differ (as do many others we have not seen), they also overlap in many ways. No art is truly unique, no matter how much it purports to be. This is because the typical human body only has two arms, two legs, and a head; and there are finite ways to utilise these appendages in combat. There are only so many ways to throw a punch or kick, and limited ways to choke, pin, and throw an opponent. *If a non-martial artist demonstrated a punch or showed what they thought would be a good way to pin someone to the floor, what do you think the results would be?* I think their efforts would produce similar results to punches and pins existing in established martial arts, albeit rough around the edges and executed poorly. There is a fair chance the punch thrown would be akin to a cross or hook, and the pin chosen would likely be the mount position. This shows that much of what many martial artists think is unique to their style is not. It is shared with other arts from around the globe, with the only real difference being executional nuance. No one has monopoly on wisdom.

The arts' roots were established in varying countries: Kung Fu (China), Karate (Japan), Wrestling (worldwide, but strongly in Africa, Middle East, and Europe), Ninjutsu (Japan), and Capoeira (Brazil). This widespread outlook on martial arts has allowed us to see how different cultures, and four of five of the inhabited continents, attempted to answer the same question. Kung Fu from China showed us how the tendrils of Buddhism played a large role in its development, and how Buddhism's lessons distilled a martial art inspired by nature. Karate and Ninjutsu from Japan demonstrated the strict, disciplined, hierarchical ways of the Japanese, which is evident in their stringent methods, resourcefulness, and focus on military efficiency. Wrestling, from around the world, allowed us to see that sometimes a culture's influence can be shunned by genetics and evolution. It showed us that regardless of religion and customs, if people are born to wrestle, they will wrestle. Lastly, Capoeira brought to light the passion, enthusiasm, and zest for life of the African people. Amidst the hardest times, we saw that rhythm, music, and personal expression can prevail with the right attitude and outlook on life – that alone is a gift worth giving and advice worth heeding.

Each of the hundreds of martial arts we have not encountered will have equally as humbling, rebellious, testing, and varied beginnings. Each will have its own story of how it came to be and why it took the form it did. A lot can be learned from the beginnings of arts, and I hope you can see there is more to an art than appears on the surface. An art is more than its punches, kicks, and grappling. Its ways tell us of the people and culture who developed it, of their history, struggles, and beliefs. Every martial art is an expression of a certain time and place, a physical embodiment of a philosophy of combat.

2

TRAINING IN MARTIAL ARTS

'Sometimes you get the bear, sometimes the bear gets you.'

Gypsy proverb

WHAT IS MARTIAL? WHAT IS ART?

Many people think of a martial art as a single entity, but I disagree. I believe martial arts consist of two separate components: the martial *and* the art. Although this is true, it is only in theory they can be considered separately, because in reality, they are inseparable. It's obvious when you think about it, as the term *martial art* tells us the two components are entirely interlocked. If you removed the *martial*, you would be left with just the *art*, or vice versa. If you care to undertake a social experiment and test the legitimacy of this theory, next time you're training or in a fight, try defending yourself with just *art*. Once you've tried it, let me know how you faired. I'll make sure to bring an icepack for your broken nose whilst you tell your story. This is because if you only study the art, you are essentially studying culture, tradition, technique, and philosophy either non-applied, or conjecturally applied to combat. This is great if theory is what you're interested in, and you have no desire to become combatively dangerous. But if this is not the case, it is well known that theory goes straight out the window when someone starts punching you in the face. Theory is important in martial arts, don't get me wrong, but it's not to be exclusively relied upon as martial arts and fighting are too practical of endeavours to be mastered by theory alone.

43

I've unfortunately fallen into this trap before, as have many martial artists bar the fortunate few. Part of starting to train in martial arts is about exploring different arts, seeing what they have to offer, and dipping in and out of different styles to see what you like, what you don't, and what suits you as an individual. I've studied many styles and concepts for varying periods of time ranging from Kung Fu, Kickboxing, Muay Thai, Ninjutsu, Mixed Martial Arts, and Jeet Kune Do. I even did a class of Wushu once – the key word here is *once*. I'm simply not built for the energetic, flexible, agile nature of the style. Five minutes into the class I thought, 'I'll leave this to the Shaolin Monks'. With my large upper body and stumpy legs, I find high kicks and jumping around not just difficult, but impractical. My body shape and size are much more suited to a grappling style such as Wrestling, because thanks to my miniature legs I have a low centre of gravity and a problem attracting women. I also have a large lung capacity thanks to my larger upper body, which means I don't gas too easily. An overly arty style (or an instructor who obsesses over the art to the detriment of the martial) will not adequately serve you in a combative situation, real or otherwise.

Whilst training Ninjutsu I spent just over a year learning techniques and movements that worked superbly in the dojo, with a compliant, friendly training partner, but proved entirely ineffective in real life. Due to the way the class was taught, there was no sparring and very little pad work – a not unusual situation in many traditional schools. This meant I was training within a context of circa 90% art, 10% martial. I felt I was making progress, and in some regards, I was. My punches and kicks were getting smoother, my stand-up grappling more fluid, and my understanding of joint manipulation was on the rise. I was also learning the really fun Ninjutsu stuff such as how to move quietly, how to wield a ninja sword, and how to control my body in mid-air – we used a trampoline. The issue was all my progress was theoretical. I was getting a feel for the Japanese culture, and I could rally off numerous techniques to an agog onlooker. But the instructor focused so heavily on the culture and traditions of Japan and Ninjutsu (which were incredibly interesting) the combative aspects I also desired were neglected. I could barely beat up a child – not that I tried. I didn't recognise this at the time as I was new to the arts. I had no idea I was focussing too intensely on the art and not sufficiently on the martial. I just assumed I was learning the way the ninja did, which made me feel much cooler than I actually am. I believed if I learned something sufficiently well in theory, when push came to shove, I would be able to apply it. I learned just how wrong I was when I took my theoretical Ninjutsu knowledge into an MMA class. Whilst sparring with a man who'd evidently eaten his vegetables as a child, I tried to apply my well-honed theoretical techniques. He'd only been training a few months, so I was more experienced than him overall, which made me feel confident about applying my knowledge. I was convinced that with a grab and a twist and a pull he'd be on the floor begging me to stop. But, as soon as I grabbed his wrist, I knew I was in too deep. He just looked at me while I held his wrist, then beat me to a pulp. That was the day I learned the martial-to-art balance mattered. It was also the day I quit Ninjutsu.

What I've just said is by no means an attack nor dismissal of Ninjutsu, but an observation in hindsight on the effectiveness of the teachings and interpretation of the style by my instructor. He was simply too arty. I say this because if you wish to achieve your potential as a martial artist, there are three components you must focus on: the style (make sure you choose a style that suits your needs), the instructor (only train under an instructor you trust, and who presents the style in a way that meets your needs – it's remarkable how different instructors interpret the same style in contrasting ways), and you (as I was once told by my instructor: 'get into martial arts or get out of it.' I can attest this is true. The path is long, meandering, time heavy, and sometimes painful, but if you don't commit to the art your progress will be stifled). By using this logic it's easy to see how much of your potential you can fulfil. For example, if you have a style that suits your needs (1 point) a bad instructor (0 points) and you put in the effort (1 point), you will score 2/3. With a quick conversion you will see in this hypothetical situation you would achieve 66% of your potential as a martial artist. *The answer to improving your score?* Simple: find a new instructor. In another example where you have a good style (1 point) a bad instructor (0 points) and you invest marginal time and effort (0 points) you will only achieve 33% of your potential. This is why it's important to try and have all three, so you can achieve the illustrious 100% potential. If we wished to be more precise in our equation, however, we would quickly find this way of thinking too simplistic because there are obvious nuances it misses. If you had a bad instructor, but they weren't completely useless, you would need to consider how bad they were. They may not be so bad to vouch a score of zero, but only good enough to score 0.25. The same can be said for the other parts of the equation. The art you're studying may be good but not perfect for you, giving it a score of 0.80. You may also fluctuate in your attendance due to outside commitments. Some weeks your effort is 1, whereas others it's 0.4, so you draw a line in the middle and give yourself 0.7. In this example you would achieve 48% of your potential.

The legendary swordsman Miyamoto Musashi in *The Book of Five Rings* wonderfully describes how the art component of martial arts is directly comparable to the art contained within other aspects of life. In the excerpt below we see how he compares the martial arts to carpentry. This perpetuates the thought that not only are the *martial* and the *art* inseparable, but that the *art* is integral for the formulation and application of the *martial*:

> *As the master carpenter is the overall organizer and director of the carpenters, it is the duty of the master carpenter to understand the regulations of the country, find out the regulations of the locality, and attend to the regulations of the master carpenter's own establishment.*

The master carpenter, knowing the measurements and designs of all sorts of structures, employs people to build houses. In this respect, the master carpenter is the same as the master warrior.

When sorting out timber for building a house, that which is straight, free from knots, and of good appearance can be used for front pillars. That which has some knots but is straight and strong can be used for rear pillars. That which is somewhat weak yet has no knots and looks good is variously used for door sills, lintels, doors and screens. That which is knotted and crooked but nevertheless strong is used thoughtfully in consideration of the strength of the various members of the house. Then the house will last a long time.

Even knotted, crooked, and weak timber can be made into scaffolding, and later used for firewood.

As the master carpenter directs the journeyman, he knows their various levels of skill and gives them appropriate tasks. Some are assigned to the flooring, some to the doors and screens, some to the sills, lintels, and ceilings, and so on. He has the unskilled set out floor joists and gets those even less skilled to carve wedges. When the master carpenter exercises discernment in the assignment of jobs, the work progresses smoothly.

Efficiency and smooth progress, prudence in all matter, recognising true courage, recognising different levels of moral, instilling confidence, and realising what can and cannot be reasonably expected – such are the matters on the mind of the master carpenter. The principle of martial arts is like this.

47

In a simplified interpretation of Musashi's text: the design, layout, and details of the house are the *art*, whereas the physical building of the house (the application of the art) is the *martial*.

The same can be said to be true if we invert our thought experiment. Try to train day in day out with just the *martial* and forgo the *art*. You would be plagued with incessant injuries which would limit your training, strain your body, and remove any type of longevity from your practice. Your technical application would be shambolic causing every sparring session to become an uncoordinated, thoughtless brawl. This brawling style of sparring is often seen when two new starters spar together, because they don't yet know the *art* (so cannot apply it) meaning they become overly dependent on the *martial*. If we push this train of thought to its eventual end, we find that becoming proficient in martial arts is nothing more than progressively learning the art whilst working on applying it.

If you overly focussed on the *martial* to the detriment of the *art*, you would never develop beyond a basic level martial artist because your training would be too damaging and aggressive. You would learn to take a beating, that's for sure, but you would never grasp nor appreciate the technicalities of the art. Modern western culture appears to have fostered an obsession with this type of purely *martial* approach in the belief it is helpful to society. It is not. Phrases such as, 'Train insane or remain the same!' are ubiquitously plastered across the internet and on gym walls to spur motivation and foster inspiration. It's definitely catchy, but as ridiculous as it sounds, just because it rhymes doesn't mean it's true. It's obvious to see that this phrase, and other akin proclamations, worship continual, full throttle exertion over sustainable practice. 'Train insane or remain the same!' Sure, by training insanely you will make shoddy short-term progress, but *can you imagine yourself being someone who will 'train insane' when you're 50, 60, or 70 years old?* If you 'train insane' (whatever that means) you are significantly more prone to injury and quitting, and the more days that pass, and the further you burn yourself out, the higher the likelihood of quitting becomes. You will most certainly quit after a few months as you become unable to maintain the 'insanity'. And with this failure to maintain 'insanity', you will lose all progress and tumble back to your old self. This would result not just in bad outcomes for your body (sprains, strains, sore joints, a bad back, etc.) but for your mind also, as you will feel like you were not good enough to 'train insane' like everyone else – who are also on the brink of quitting but too ashamed to admit it. I'm sure you will agree that the phrase would be much more accurate if it declared 'train insane *and* remain the same!'. Massaki Hatsumi verbalises the same opinion, although much more elegantly when he says, 'There's an appropriate way to train when you're young and vigorous. There's a proper way to train when you enter the advanced years of your life. There's an appropriate way to train when you're sick, and there's a proper way to train when it seems no workout works... Constant training, always adjusting the goal to the means at hand at your disposal, is the only way to cultivate the true strength that transcends all limitations'.

The same could be said about the western world's stigmatisation of sleep and how stopping working has become viewed as a weakness as opposed to an integral part of sustainable longevity. There appears to be a societal drive for ceaselessly increased productivity and working extra hours in your free time (attractively labelled as a 'side hustle') to generate more income. This is an incredibly complex topic that feeds into, and from, politics, sociology, technology, and economics. I will not attempt to tackle its complexity here as it's of no benefit to the book, but this concerningly *martial* approach to the work/rest balance increasingly leaves everybody with fewer hours for sleep and the negative impact that brings. In Matthew Walker's ironically eye-opening book, *Why We Sleep*, he puts forward a robust, thought-provoking defence of sleep. The most poignant takeaway from his book is that the shorter you sleep, the shorter your life span. Phrases such as 'you can sleep when you're dead' and 'sleep is for the weak' have attempted to nullify this finding, with a concerning level of success. Dare I say in some circles it is now considered 'cool' if you have suppressed your need for sleep in the pursuit of goals, money, and glory. It also doesn't help that some famous people and social media influencers tow this line, either completely unaware (maybe due to a lack of sleep), or knowingly dismissive of its dangers. Sleep is the most effective thing we can do to reset our brain and body health each day. *Can you imagine training into your golden years without a healthy brain and body?* I thought not. It's also true we can never sleep back that which we have previously lost. A chronic lack of sleep, or a long-term broken sleep pattern, will catch up with you down the line no matter how much you sleep in later months and years. This is something I wish I had known earlier. If you continue to work and train too hard for too long without sufficient rest, no matter your age, you will eventually exhibit physical ailments, mental health instability, reduced alertness, and impaired memory. All of which will prove to be significant hurdles to progression and sustainability in martial arts training, as well as other areas of life. There's much more to this topic if you're interested enough to delve into it, but don't stay up too late reading about it. If you want to train for your entire life then sleep, nap, don't drink too much alcohol or caffeine, have a good diet, listen to your body, exercise, balance the *martial* with the *art*, and ignore all the bullshit that points to the contrary. Too *martial* an approach to anything, not just martial arts, is detrimental to progress. We would be better as a society to exalt phrases such as, 'If you're moving, you're improving!' or, 'Train in a way that lets you train forever!'. The key to success is to train sustainably, and for that, you need the *art*.

If you adopted a purely *martial* approach to your training, you would also never achieve many of the finer refinements of martial arts, such as the state of fluidity, understanding, and biomechanical autonomy known as *Mushin*. Mushin literally means *mind without mind*. It's a state free from discursive thought, a state of emptiness where your body unconsciously reacts to the movements of your opponent instead of requiring you to process what is happening, formulate a response, and cognitively respond. Most professional fighters and long-term martial artists achieve (or have achieved) Mushin at some point, but it doesn't come easy. It takes years of focussed, consistent, dedicated practice to achieve such a level. Bruce Lee famously proclaimed his state of Mushin when he said, 'When the opponent expands, I contract. When he contracts, I expand. And when there is an opportunity, I do not hit – [my fist] hits all by itself'. The legendary Zen master, Takuan Sōhō, also wrote on Mushin and why it is important in combat. Some of you may have seen the below passage before because it is an oft-quoted text when these types of things are discussed. Either way, it aptly and poetically describes how Mushin is an invaluable state of being that can only be achieved from combined *martial* and *art* refinement:

The mind must always be in the state of 'flowing', for when it stops anywhere that means the flow is interrupted and it is this interruption that is injurious to the well-being of the mind. In the case of the swordsman, it means death.

When the swordsman stands against his opponent, he is not to think of the opponent, nor of himself, nor of his enemy's sword movements. He just stands there with his sword which, forgetful of all technique, is ready only to follow the dictates of the subconscious. The man has effaced himself as the wielder of the sword. When he strikes, it is not the man but the sword in the hand of the man's subconscious that strikes.

Sōhō's description shows us that to become a high-level martial artist, the *art* is integral. It is not just about punching bags, sparring, and fighting until someone quits. Real, long-term progress is about balance. It's about establishing a sustainable equilibrium between both the *martial* and the *art*. The *martial* on its own is simply too hard, and the *art*, too soft. They are the yin and yang of combat. They need each other to survive, because on their own, they are effectively useless.

THE MARTIAL TO ART BALANCE

What's the correct balance between the martial and the art? How do you ensure your training has longevity without being combatively useless? How do you ensure you don't get injured too much, or broken too soon? Well, as you may expect, the answer is: it depends.

When we look at the traditional martial arts (Kung Fu, Karate, Ninjutsu, Capoeira, Wrestling, Fencing, Pankration, Muay Thai, etc.) it's obvious to see that some are more martial, whereas others are more arty. *But why is this?* There are many factors to consider when it comes to scrutinising the formulation of a martial art that was created in cultural isolation. For instance, *what sort of societal structure was in place when the martial art was born?* If we look at the Japanese martial arts (Karate, Ninjutsu, etc.) we see they are strict, regimented, and hierarchical, which is a direct reflection of the society the arts were born into. Traditionally, you would not dare to question a Japanese sensei, for the repercussions would be painful and instantaneously regrettable. At the time of the inception of these arts, Japanese culture demanded everyone knew their place, and that honour, respect, and loyalty were embraced. We can see these societal traits in Karate and Ninjutsu by the way they are taught, trained, and applied. The arts are a physical incarnation of their host culture. On the contrary, if we look at an art like Capoeira, which we have seen already in the beginning of the book, we will see the art was born from a society with much less emphasis on social class – yes, the Africans were slaves, but the art was created within the slave's sub-society, not the Brazilian society as a whole, where social stratification was much less evident. As a result, Capoeira's movements are freer, the style more liberal, and the relationship between master and student much less regimented than in Japan. There are also rhythms, philosophies, and instruments in Capoeira that link it back to its founder's African heritage, especially Angola. It's all there for us to see, we just need to look close enough. The same is true for all other martial arts. Muay Thai, from Thailand, is illustrative of Thai society; Fencing, from France, an embodiment of French society; and Kali, for the Philippines, an expression of Filipino society. Dan Inosanto, the highly respected martial artist and head instructor at the Inosanto Academy, California, has publicly proclaimed on many occasions that martial arts are a great way to immerse yourself in varying cultures. By studying martial arts from different cultures, you will not just learn to defend yourself, you will receive an insight into how other cultures live, think, and function. He is a staunch believer that if more people studied martial arts there would be less cultural friction in the world, more understanding and empathy, and stronger international relationships. I could not agree more.

Another strongly influencing factor is the level of threat a region was under at the time the martial art was born. If the threat level was high, the martial art would be more likely to be aggressive, and if it was low, the art would have a higher chance of being placid and playful. It's also worth pointing out that martial arts born and used in isolation can evolve from their initial form, and if an environment becomes safer and more peaceful, a martial art can drift dangerously far into the arty sphere as the martial side becomes less required. The same can be said for the opposite. This means when a martial art is considered in isolation, some form of preservation is integral to its ongoing effectiveness, otherwise, the art may be in danger of getting watered-down as society becomes peaceful. There's a great saying that strongly applies to this could-be watering down process: 'The first generation of martial artists are fighters, the second are technicians, and the third live off the reputation of the first and the second.'

It can also be seen that arts born into dangerous regions are more martial in their approach than those born into passivity, but not exclusively. Examples of martial arts likely born into turmoil are Muay Thai, Karate, and Kali – sometimes called Arnis or Escrima. Each of these arts are considered effective, and in some instances, almost to the point of devastation. Try picking a fight with a good Muay Thai fighter and you will soon understand the validity of this point. Muay Thai (also known as the science of eight limbs as it uses both hands, elbows, knees, and feet as weapons) was an art used in war. It was an art devised for self-defence, self-offense, the protection of elephants (elephants were used in ancient Thailand to transport possessions and people of value) and killing. Muay Thai is a simple art when compared to many others. But, regardless of its simplicity, it is brutally effective.

If we look at Karate and Kali, we will find the same. Karate, as we have seen, was developed on the Okinawa prefecture as a means of self-defence. Kali, whose beginnings are difficult to trace, was likely born into tribalism and used by the poor in lawless lands. Kali is an energy and movement efficient art that holds nothing back and intends to maim and kill. It employs an arsenal of weapons (large sticks, short sticks, swords, and myriad knives) alongside boxing and other techniques that make your eyes water. Its effectiveness was proven when the Spanish invaded the Philippines in 1521 before being slaughtered at the hands of the bellicose Filipino farmers.

If we flipped this situation and looked at arts born into peaceful times (or which have evolved out of their combative states and into more theoretical forms) we would find them much artier, and in a lot of instances, much less militarily effective. This doesn't diminish their value, however, as the partial shunning of the martial in pursuit of the art can make them vestiges of culture and tradition – as long as they don't drift too far from their original form. It just requires us to look at them differently and no longer approach them as if they are fully effective fighting systems. Styles such as Wushu and Tai Chi provide evidence of this. It would be unfair to proclaim these styles entirely ineffective in combat (well, perhaps not Tai Chi), but it would be reasonable to say that compared to other arts that were born into warfare or maintained their original combative forms, these arts would suffer if they competed with one another.

We see a similar process happening today where martial arts are being transformed into sports. The difference in this situation is that instead of an art becoming less martial and more arty, the art's original form is being sacrificed in the name of sport. This doesn't necessarily make an art non-combatively effective (many combat sports are more effective than real martial arts) but it does take away some of the art's edge, and its techniques designed for fighting without rules. Brazilian Jiu Jitsu is an example of this. There are two main forms of Brazilian Jiu Jitsu today: sport Jiu Jitsu, and combat or street Jiu Jitsu. Sport Jiu Jitsu, which is majority managed and influenced by the IBJJF (International Brazilian Jiu Jitsu Federation) is currently undergoing, in the eyes of many practitioners, a watering-down process. This is because the IBJJF are banning certain techniques (slicers and heel hooks for example) and forcing the sport version of the martial art down a points-based scoring route. This, many practitioners say, is pulling the art away from its original purpose whilst making it safer and less combatively effective.

The above points all focus on external factors that have influenced the creation of a martial art, but we can also look inwardly to see why a certain martial art may be more martial or arty by focusing on who conceived it in the first place. Internal factors such as the gender of the person may matter – most martial arts have been devised by men, but a few have been created by women, the most famous of which is Wing Chun. The founder of Wing Chun, Ng Mui, was said to have created the art as she did not find the large, powerful movements of other Shaolin Kung Fu styles suitable for her more fragile physique. Her small stature and weaker muscles required something more subtle than grandiose kicks and large circular punches. This is why Wing Chun is based upon the redirection of force and the manipulation of limbs (known as trapping) whilst also placing a large emphasis on direct, short, straight punches that are thrown in succession (known as chain punches or Lin Wan Kuen) as opposed to the larger hooks and uppercuts found in most other styles. In Wing Chun the kicks are also much smaller when compared to other styles and place more emphasis on being direct and targeted towards weak areas such as the kneecap.

Other internal factors we could consider are, *was the person old or young? What was the individual's mentality? Were they a peaceful monk?* As is the case with the majority of Kung Fu styles. *Or a person set on suppressing an underclass to maintain their own social status?* Such as the samurai. What about, *did the person feel the style needed to be deadly in the first place?* Such as Ninjutsu. *Or was it simply a way to defeat an opponent, but not necessarily kill them?* Like many styles of Wrestling. *What was the person's body size? Did they focus predominantly on defeating larger opponents because they were small? Or were they sufficiently large meaning size was an inherent advantage, so less focus needed to be placed on leverage and physics and more could be targeted on strength and power?* The list of potential questions is large, but without asking them all I feel the point has been made.

As we can see there are myriad variables to consider when asking: *what is the correct martial to art balance?* And the answer truly is: it depends. It depends on the person studying. *Who are they? Where are they from? What is their temperament? Are they genetically strong or fast? How long are their limbs? What do they need the martial art for? What environment do they live in? How often are they likely to use it? How old are they? Do they have to learn it quickly or can it be a longer educational process?* In the end, martial arts of varying *martial* to *art* balances can be effective, just as long as one is not embraced to the detriment of the other.

MIND, BODY, AND SPIRIT

All martial arts, regardless of origin, style, or purpose, focus on developing three main areas: mind, body, and spirit. This is true to such an extent that even arts that do not specifically intend to develop and refine these areas do so as an unintended by-product. If you're an experienced martial artist who has consumed a reasonably wide breadth of martial arts literature, at this point you're probably thinking, 'here we go, another book ranting about the warrior code and how to become a modern-day warrior… blah blah blah'. Well, you'll be glad to hear this is not my intent, and I wish to proffer thoughts, opinions, and empirical findings based more along the lines of modern-day thinking and application. So please, give me the benefit of the doubt.

Firstly, we'll take a brief look at the mind.

In martial arts, the mind is required for four major things.

One, to digest the art, techniques, and philosophies so they can be practiced, refined, and applied in combat – competition or otherwise. The ability to digest what you're being taught, understand it, and apply it, are of obvious importance in martial arts. This first part of the mind's development feeds back into the section above where we spoke of the *martial* to *art* balance. There must be sufficient dedication to the *art* aspect of the martial art if you wish to master these things. Techniques must be practiced thousands of times if you're to fully understand them. You must also ensure you have balance between your training and non-training lives so you can rest, recuperate, and get enough sleep. This enables your mind to recover and distil the lessons it has been taught. It allows your brain to move the knowledge and experiences from its short-term memory to its long-term memory, which makes them available when you need them next. Without sufficient practice and rest you would never adequately develop your mind in this area.

Two, to control the thoughts, fears, and anger inherent in a martial discipline. I'm sure we've all been in a situation where anger or fear have taken over, leaving the mind clouded and judgment skewed. This type of situation is of benefit to no one, especially the person experiencing the intense emotions. This is especially true when applied to a combative situation. 'Anger just makes people inefficient' says martial arts coach, John Danaher, 'their breathing gets shallow, they're too muscularly tense; they gas fast'. It only takes a little imagination to see that tensing up, clouding your judgment, and burning yourself out too quickly are bad for fighting. Clarity and stillness of mind are of gargantuan value in stressful, angry, fearful situations – if you have the ability to achieve them. It's true that by exposing yourself to mock combative situations such as competitions, you will enable yourself to experience these emotions in a controlled setting. Competitions will give you the opportunity to bask in these emotions and see how they really make you feel, and to learn how your mind responds when under pressure. As with everything we are discussing here, this point is of great importance to martial arts, because martial arts are often trained as a safeguarding mechanism to be employed during times of intense stress and fear. The more you are taken outside your comfort zone, the better skilled you will be at controlling your emotions, reducing anxiety, and sensibly working through the situation.

Three, to understand the strategy that is specific to the person's chosen martial art, as well as being able to decipher what strategies are best suited to the individual given their current strengths and weaknesses. Strategy is often overlooked in martial arts training, as too many instructors simply rely on teaching techniques, whilst not focusing sufficiently on the technique's application in the bigger picture. It's important a student of the art understands not just what they can do given their skillset, but when is the best time to do these things, in what order, and how the strategic process is beneficial. As with all strategies, they must be flexible, adaptable, and multi-layered. This is one of the advantages sports fighting has over non-sport martial arts. Almost all sports fighting employs the study of strategy, because to not do so would most certainly mean failure in competition. Whereas traditional, non-sporting martial arts often unwittingly omit this integral development aspect, therefore leaving not just holes in their students' capabilities, but a whole section of the mind undeveloped. Imagine an Olympic wrestler or judoka stepping forth to fight for their country without a strategy. It just wouldn't happen. Understanding the strengths and weaknesses of your art (yes, all arts have weaknesses) and yourself will enable you to plan better and fight more effectively. Just as understanding how your knowledge fits together and how it is best applied in a given situation will increase your likelihood of success.

Four, to learn to see the bigger picture of the art so you can make the art your own and not simply regurgitate your instructor's interpretation. 'My job is to first make you see the things to which you are currently blind' says John Danaher, 'then to make you see all that I see, and ultimately to make you see further than I ever did.' This superb quote shows exactly why the mind is such an important tool in studying, refining, and developing the martial arts. Without the use of the mind both the martial art and the martial artist would stagnate, before eventually falling out of existence. With good training the mind provides knowledge and focus, wisdom and clarity, all of which are integral weapons in the arsenal of a good martial artist. All martial arts journeys are started by doing exactly what you're told and copying your instructor – of course they are, there is no other way. But once the art is grasped and understood, the student should look to make the art fit them, and no longer work on making themselves fit the art. This may sound simple, but as the mind is fragile and open to influence it is a slow and delicate process. 'The mind is like a fertile garden', Bruce Lee once said, 'it will grow anything you wish to plant – beautiful flowers or weeds'.

So, make sure you plant flowers. Be open to suggestion, question what you think you know, be creative, and once you understand the art sufficiently make it your own.

The second aspect of personal development is the body. The best way to think of the body is as the antithesis of the mind. This places the mind and body into a yin and yang style relationship. The mind and body are both required if someone wishes to succeed within martial arts, so it is important that within the development of the mind, the body is utilised (technique repetition, being able to undertake the physical tasks required to fulfil a mental strategy), and the development of the body is also reinforced through the use of the mind (motivation, focus, and discipline). It's very cliché, I agree, and I know it's easy to switch off when someone starts to talk about yin and yang and other ancient martial arts principles. But in this instance, the application of yin and yang is ideal. Even though the body and mind can be considered separately, they are both required, and each must contain a small amount of the other to flourish. The body and mind are comparable to the *martial* and the *art* we encountered earlier. The mind contains the *art,* but the body is required to apply the *art* to the *martial.*

The body can be trained in two ways: martially and artily. As we have seen above, a good balance between the two is important, but the balance required depends on myriad variables which must be assessed and ascertained by both the martial art and the martial artist. The easiest way to look at this is by dividing the bodily attributes required into the two specified categories.

The martial: strength, speed, flexibility, power, agility, cardiovascular fitness, muscular endurance, pain threshold, mobility, tendon strength, etc.

The art: coordination, timing, reflex, sensitivity, rhythm, balance, bodily awareness, etc.

Everyone will have their own unique makeup from the constituents above. I'm not saying everyone has these things in good measure, but they will exist in some quantities. For example, you may have good strength, coordination, and cardiovascular fitness, but poor rhythm and flexibility. Everyone will differ. But even if these qualities are only possessed in infinitesimal amounts, they are still possessed, and can therefore be trained and developed. This means it's important the martial artist takes stock of their strengths and weaknesses and focuses on developing themselves to their full physical potential. If someone is naturally strong, they may be able to limit their strength training and focus more on their weaker areas such as flexibility and timing. If they are naturally flexible, they may be able to stretch infrequently as their flexibility requires little maintenance, but they have to spend a significant amount of time working on their balance. With targeted training, the martial artist's bodily attributes will improve, which will lead to noticeable enhancements in their physical performance. Some schools incorporate physical training strategies into their regimes, focusing on the components most valuable to the art. Others prefer to focus purely on the application of the art (which will improve some of the physical qualities required via training) but leave the real physical development for the individual to manage themselves. There is no right or wrong way to do this. As with everything, the key is balance and sustainability. As long as the body is being developed in some way, progress will be made. A martial artist should devise and frequently review their routine in such a way that it remains sustainable for the rest of their life. It's not possible to train at 70 years old like you did at 20, so changing your physical conditioning routine to accommodate these changes is important. There is nothing to be gained from trying to maintain the same routine for years on end. Life changes, you change, and your priorities change, so ensure your physical training changes with you.

The development of the body is another area sometimes overlooked by the non-sporting arts, but never by the sporting arts. No competitive wrestler, boxer, Thai boxer, or judoka is out of shape, because they operate within real combative situations. The consequences of being an out of shape combat sports athlete are not worth considering. But the same is not always true for the non-sporting arts that can be more theoretical. It should be, but it's not. Even if you don't compete you should place a large focus on improving your physicality. Your body is the means by which you express the art, and a weak body will only result in a poor expression. God forbid, if there ever comes a moment when you need to use your skills for real, I'm sure you'll agree you'd want your body to be in prime physical condition so you can express your art as powerfully as possible.

Lastly, we have the spirit. The spirit is certainly the most esoteric of the three areas we are discussing but is nonetheless an integral part of martial arts training. As with the mind and body, some people inherently have stronger spirits than others. This can be accredited to myriad variables such as upbringing, genetics, experiences, and mentality – all of which can play an integral role in the strengthening (or weakening) of the spirit. Many people are inclined to believe the spirit is strengthened with age, because the spirit sounds and feels like something wise and mature, but this is most certainly not the case. In many instances, the opposite can be true, and a person's spirit can become weaker as they age due to factors like traumatic experiences or a soft lifestyle, which almost all of us in the west are guilty of. This point is reinforced by the fact there are strong spirited children and weak spirited adults.

This leaves us with the question: *how does one strengthen the spirit?* Traditionally, martial artists looked to strengthen the spirit through activities such as meditation and introspection. Meditation is used to calm the mind by clearing it of negative and intrusive thoughts. It is used to focus the mind, erase peripheral noise, and achieve a sense of calm and composure that can hopefully be carried day to day. Introspection is a means by which a martial artist can scrutinise, question, and shape themselves. Through introspection it is possible to learn about your mental strengths and weaknesses, your preferences and fears. Knowing oneself is an almost impossible task, however, as one changes with time and experience meaning you are always playing catchup. Introspection could be compared to learning to care for a new-born baby. At first you know nothing, but soon you figure out what the baby likes and dislikes, when it likes to sleep and what each of the noises mean. As soon as you've figured this out though, the baby has grown and changed. Now its noises are all different and its likes and dislikes have changed meaning you have to figure everything out again. You have experience with the baby now, which makes things a little easier, but you still need to learn the baby's ways again each time it changes. This is exactly what introspection is like; a continual chasing of yourself in the hope you will momentarily know who you are.

Today, these techniques are still used by some, especially meditation, which has shown itself to be scientifically beneficial and is making a fashionable comeback via apps such as Headspace and Calm. But in my eyes, although meditation and introspection can be effective, they can also be considered purely *arty* when we think about them on the *martial* to *art* spectrum. This can lead to a false sense of security because the spirit has only been trained within a theoretical context, so once the shit hits the fan and the peaceful world of meditation and introspection are left behind, *will you be able to keep your spirit strong?* I personally don't think so. I think the arty benefits gained from meditation and introspection need to be paired with something more *martial* if they are to be effective. I believe once the theoretical benefits of meditation and introspection have been gained, it is advantageous to fight. You need to place yourself into a stressful, high adrenaline environment whilst trying to use the lessons learned from your meditation and introspection. You need to test your spirit under pressure, and only then will you know its strength. It doesn't matter if the fighting is in competition (although I would state this is the most effective), in class, or during some at home training with a partner. The thing that matters most is that *emotional intensity* is invested in the fight. As you can imagine, the most emotionally intense way to fight is for real, but this is obviously not a viable option. 'What's important' says Forrest Morgan, author of *Living the Martial Way*, 'is you must have both the will and ability to do in a crisis what your art attempts to teach you in the training hall.' That is why I favour competitions, as they are as close to the emotionally straining, anxiety inducing, fear breeding thing as we can get without seriously putting our health on the line. This shows if you compete regularly, push yourself beyond your comfort zone, and meditate and make time for introspection, you will strengthen your spirit and learn about yourself.

There are also other ways of martially strengthening the spirit such as katas – practicing movements alone. If the kata is rehearsed with sufficient emotional intensity the spirit will be strengthened over time. To achieve this benefit though, each strike must be committed to, and every movement performed confidently You must feel the intent in every punch, kick, and block. You must believe in the power and application of each movement. But many modern schools choose to omit katas for a couple of reasons. One their art has not developed in such a way that katas can be used Two, emotionally intensive sparring is generally considered more effective as it provides a more combative experience, which is o greater benefit to the student's spirit.

It can be seen there are different ways to train the spirit just as there are varying ways to train the mind and body. Some ar more effective than others, but all work in some way. The main thing is that whatever method is used, emotional intensity must b applied, and a balance between the *martial* and the *art* should b achieved.

TRAINING

We have seen thus far that many arts arose around the globe contrasting environments, some earlier than others, mar simultaneously, and multiple for differing reasons. But even thoug many arts were born into isolation, the methods and techniques used to train and refine them significantly overlap. After all, considering most martial artists are more physically and biologically alike than they are different, it's no surprise there are finite ways to develop oneself.

Almost all training methods can be considered on the *Isolate and Apply* Scale – see *Figure.1*

Figure.1 – Isolate and Apply Scale

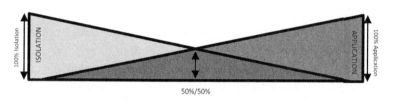

50%/50%

The left-hand-side of *Figure.1* represents 100% isolation, whereas the right-hand-side represents 100% application. We can see as we move from left to right, isolation decreases, and application increases. If we look at the centre of the figure, we can see that due to the decrease in isolation and increase in application, we are now at a 50%/50% point where both are being used in equal measure. If we continue to move to the right-hand-side of the figure we can see isolation tails off and application now becomes predominant.

Due to the subjectivity of martial arts, there will be inherent differences in opinion as to how isolated or applied a training method is considered to be. All I wish to do here is explain a few main training methods and proffer my opinion as to where these would approximately sit on the *Isolate and Apply Scale*. You may disagree with some of my opinions, which is more than fine, as training methods are always open to scrutiny. But I hope you will find the scale useful when thinking of your training and quantifying

65

how much isolated practice or real application you are doing. I say this because by looking at things this way you may realise you are focusing too heavily on isolation, and if you want to make gains in you training you may have to incorporate more application of what you've learnt. The opposite may be true. You may feel you are constantly failing to apply what you have learnt in sparring because your technique is sloppy. This could be a sign you need to minimise or remove the application for this technique and focus on training it in a more isolated manner for a while. There is no set way to train, as different arts, instructors, and students will feel happier training at differing points on the scale. But it is a tool to use to help quantify and gauge your training.

I feel it's also important I state that methods of training which occupy all positions on the scale are of benefit. It's not the case that 100% application is better than 70% isolation and 30% application, or any other combination. It is important to the development of a martial artist that their training occupies many positions on the scale depending on their needs.

For the sake of context, I will be considering 100% isolation as the training of a technique in an environment completely removed from an opponent or training partner, or any type of physical contact or interaction. I will be considering 100% application as the full-blown application of everything a martial artist knows. In other words: sparring.

We will start on the isolation end of the scale and work our way along.

DISCUSSION

Figure.2 – Isolate and Apply Scale, Discussion

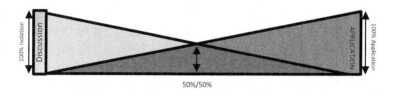

Discussion is an often-overlooked aspect of training. But anyone who's been a member of a gym for a reasonable time will tell you there are instances (sometimes long instances) where the students and instructor stand around discussing a technique's application. These discussions often start when a beginner asks, *why do you do that?* Or *could I not just punch you in the face?* Other times the instructor breaks into a protracted monolog, or a more experienced student wishes to dig deeper into a technique to help them grasp its nuances. Whatever the reason may be, discussion should, and often does, form a reasonable part of martial arts training.

As you would imagine, discussion occupies a place on the *Isolate and Apply Scale* that is 100% isolation. There is no application of discussion. You can't choke someone unconscious with a discussion – although you could bore them to death. Discussion is integral for all martial artists. It allows thoughts to be aired, ideas to be exchanged, theories to be tested, knowledge to be refined, and the art itself to be greater understood. *Why does your foot move to that position when you kick? Why does your lead arm swing across your centreline when you throw a round kick? How do I greater stabilise my base when I'm in top side control so I can maximise top pressure and minimise my chances of being swept?* Without discussion these questions would never be answered, and your martial arts would remain unrefined and slapdash.

So, embrace discussion like an old friend. Talk through your thoughts, no matter how silly they feel. An idea or concept that seems evidently obvious to you may be revolutionary to someone else. But don't get trapped in a state of permanent discussion because theory will only take you so far. If you wish to be a truly great martial artist, you need to learn to apply what you have learnt.

KATAS

Figure.3 – Isolate and Apply Scale, Katas

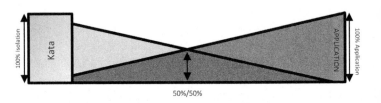

A Kata is a series of movements performed alone in thin air. There are varying difficulties of katas ranging from short routines containing 10 repeated moves, to highly complex katas containing hundreds of techniques which require serious skill and athleticism to complete. Katas tend to be used in the traditional striking arts such a Kung-Fu and Karate as a means of training a technique to technical perfection. They are also used for the strengthening of the spirit when emotional intensity is applied, and the development of strength, speed, flexibility, coordination, and a host of other valuable attributes. Katas are frequently used in gradings where a student will perform a set kata (amongst other things) to show they are sufficiently skilled to be promoted to the next belt. The higher the belt, the more complex the kata performed.

The great thing about katas is they can be performed completely alone. This makes them quite unique in martial arts because a lot of martial arts training is understandably reliant on having a training partner. Due to this, they are a complete isolation of techniques. Whilst performing a kata a student may focus on the technique's application and deliver each block or blow with focus and intent. But the application imagined whilst performing a kata alone is purely theoretical making them a 100% isolation training technique.

There is such a thing as a paired kata, however. This is where two people practice their techniques together in a set routine – sort of like a dance. As one person throws a punch, the other will evade or block it using a predetermined technique, and so on. The paired kata method of training does have more application than a solo kata because there are energies being felt from another person as you use your techniques. But paired katas are still highly isolated training methods as they do not allow any real application of technique in an uncertain or live setting. This is why in *Figure.3* you will see katas do reach out of the 100% isolation section and into the small percentages of application, but only marginally.

FLOWS & ENERGY DRILLS

Figure.4 – Isolate and Apply Scale, Flows & Energy Drills

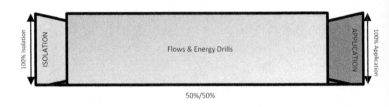

Flows and energy drills are one of my personal favourite ways to train. They're creative, fun, interactive, and can be tweaked to meet the skillset and training demands of the individual. They're a great way to gain technique repetition without getting bored, and they're just like playing, which is always a bonus. This is why they occupy such a large space on the *Isolate and Apply Scale* – see *Figure.4*.

Lots of arts tie techniques together into circuitous flows or energy drills which enables the two participating individuals to perform a continual cycle containing a set number of predetermined techniques. This enables each technique contained within the cycle to be practiced many times in a flowing environment, whilst allowing the participants to continually feel their opponent's energy. Participants can choose to undertake the flow slowly (therefore focusing on technique) or quickly – once the flow is known, and therefore focusing more on reflex and muscle memory. There is also the option of adding techniques into these pre-established flows which increases their application and makes them infinitely more complex – so complex in some instances that simply watching them hurts your brain. Sometimes the flows have no pre-set structure, and the students simply react to one another in the way they see fit – this is especially common in the grappling arts where they call this *flow roll*. The idea of a flow roll is to allow the participants to m only test their techniques in a safe, controlled environment, but to also find what techniques are ingrained in muscle memory and how quick their reflexes are. Flow rolls are a fantastic way of training – as long as they're not undertaken by two people who are too competitive which inevitably escalates and results in a full grappling match and battle for victory. There is a lot of creativity to be found in this area of training, which is why it's so fun and engaging.

A couple of examples of flows and energy drills are *Hubud* and *Punyo Sumbrada* from Kali, and *Chi Sau* or *Sticky Hands* from Wing Chun. Within the grappling arts a sweep, lock, escape, sweep… flow may be used, or any other combination of techniques the students wish to cluster together and practice. Even in the oldest fighting style of them all, Wrestling, there is an energy drill called *pummelling*. This is essentially a standing hug with your training partner, where you have one arm on the outside of the hug and the other on the inside. You then pummel by moving your outside arm to the inside of the hug whilst your partner does the same, which leaves you still in a hug position but with your arms in the opposite positions to which you began. From this position, grabs, takedowns, locks, and throws can be inserted so you get a better feel for your opponent and how to manipulate them from a set reference point.

PAD WORK

Figure.5 – Isolate and Apply Scale, Pad Work

Pad work has the potential to cover almost all the *Isolate and Apply Scale* (see *Figure.5*) with the exception of its very peripherals – just like the flows and energy drills training we encountered a moment ago. With sufficient creativity, pad work can help a striking martial artist of any level in nearly all aspects of their training.

Let's say you've just started Kickboxing and you want to isolate a simple, singular technique – a jab. Your coach dons their focus mitts, raises one hand, and awaits the impact of your jab. Whilst throwing your jab, you focus on your mechanics. *Is your punching hand turned over enough? How's your footwork? Are you dropping your rear hand each time you throw the jab?* Each of these things can be observed by both you and your coach whilst you work your jab. Your coach may notice a few flaws in your technique, so they make some recommendations to improve it. You may feel a little uncomfortable as you move, so you play with your body and arm position until it feels smooth and natural. After training this way for a while you will develop a strong, technically solid jab. Your technique will be good, your jab nice and sharp, and your timing and rhythm like clockwork. But as you will agree, this is a very isolated way of training the jab with just a smidgen of application thrown in. If you felt your jab was good and you wished to increase the level of application, you could focus on moving off centreline once you've thrown your jab, or your coach could start to move around you forcing you to throw your jab towards a moving object whilst also focusing on your footwork. Each of these changes complicates the process of throwing a jab, which greater increases the application of the technique in a progressively more realistic way.

If we wished to move a little further from the isolation end of the scale and integrate more application, all we would have to do is make the pad work more combative. There are many ways to do this, of which we have just seen one example above with the jab. Other ways to achieve more application are: combining multiple techniques, introducing more movement and therefore footwork, and allowing the pad holder to throw strikes at you in between completed combinations – or if you're really wanting to go harder on yourself then allow the pad holder to retort mid-combination. It's also possible to have the pad holder throw one of a few agreed techniques at the end of your combination, and each technique will have an agreed upon, pre-trained response. For example, once you've finished throwing your combination, the pad holder may come back with a jab, which means you must parry the jab with your rear hand whilst returning a lead knee followed by a push and a leg kick. Or they could throw a right leg round kick, which means you catch the leg and take them to the floor before delivering some ground and pound and passing their guard. If you wanted to really mix it up, once you've finished your combination the pad holder could pull out a knife, which you would then disarm before taking them to the floor and choking them. The list is endless, meaning the only limit to this style of training is your creativity.

Pad work is a truly great way to train when done intelligently and with intent. I believe this to such an extent that I would say you are missing out on a whole dimension of training if you don't do it. Pad work can help you master a single technique on your first day or allow you to powerfully execute years of knowledge in a combative setting – and everything in between. This is why many arts from Karate and Kung Fu to Muay Thai and Taekwondo frequently use pad work as a means of training their arts. It's tried, it's tested, and it's effective.

SPARRING

Figure.6 – Isolate and Apply Scale, Sparring

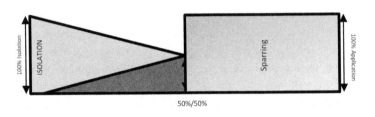

Lastly, we will take a look at sparring, which is the truest essence of applied martial arts. Although sparring is as close as you can get to the real application of martial arts in a truly threatening situation, it can be tweaked and played with to aid a martial artist's development.

There are three main types of sparring (their names differ according to which art you study but they are essentially the same): touch sparring, semi-contact, and full contact. The grappling arts are an exception to this, however, as almost all sparring in grappling arts is undertaken as full contact. There are instances where lighter sparring is seen in the grappling arts (we explored them above when we discussed flow rolls), but on the whole, the grappling arts go full contact because it is often safer for them to do so than it is in the striking arts. This is one of the advantages grappling arts have over striking arts – they can be practiced more realistically more frequently.

Touch sparring is exactly as it sounds – you simply touch your opponent very lightly. Some arts fully orientate themselves around this type of sparring (they sometimes call it points sparring) where the aim is to touch your opponent with a strike and if you do, you score a point. This isn't the only situation in which touch sparring is found, however, as more aggressive arts such as MMA and Muay Thai also sometimes utilise touch sparring as a way of allowing practitioners to take more risks and isolate techniques without the fear of getting their teeth knocked out.

Semi-contact is also exactly as it sounds – sparring using circa 50% power. This style of sparring is more realistic and aggressive than touch sparring and therefore has a higher level of application. Semi-contact sparring is just like a real sporting fight, you just don't try and knock each other unconscious.

Full contact sparring (as you've undoubtedly guessed by now) is sparring with everything you have. It's the purest essence of applied martial arts within a safe (often refereed) environment. In full contact sparring the aim of the game is to hurt the other person. You want to either knock them out, down, or force them to quit. In the grappling arts, the aim of full contact sparring is often to either pin (Wrestling), submit (BJJ), or throw (Judo) your opponent. As you can imagine, full contact sparring is intense, and is as close as you can get to real fighting without seriously putting yourself at risk. There are of course limitations to sparring such as rules, round timings, and illegal moves; so, sparring is not considered real combat – this is something to be very aware of when training for self-defence purposes as overconfidence in sparring can make one complacent. In fact, with a little scrutiny it can be seen that sparring is actually more orientated around cooperation than competition – stay with me. Let's use an MMA bout as an example. When two fighters face one another in a cage they have agreed to cooperate on many things before they fight. The have agreed to be bound by the rules of the sport (which means no illegal moves), the timing of the rounds, the maximum duration the fight can go, and the decisions of the referee and score cards. The fighters agree they will only compete (and they will compete fiercely) within these boundaries, and they understand if they break these rules they will be punished. This competition within the agreed parameters of cooperation does not exist outside the training hall or sports arena, which is a very important note for all martial artists. Saying this, however, sparring (especially full contact sparring) is the best way there is to test your skills relatively safely and will likely make you formidable in a real fighting situation.

What we have seen are just a few examples of some of the main training methods used across martial arts. Many others exist (some of which will be unique to certain arts), but we can clearly see that although many arts were devised in isolation, many of their predominant training methods and philosophies overlap.

Once you become consumed by martial arts it becomes evident you must work on all aspects of yourself if you wish to improve. This is a by-product of a truly holistic process. Both past and present-day martial artists understand they must not just harness a thorough understanding of the art but must undertake physical training to aid performance alongside mental preparation for when the art needs to be realistically applied. And the more martial art seep into people's lives, the more omnipresent their ways become. Martial arts can be seen everywhere. Two people hugging forms a grappling reference point. *Where are their arms placed during the hug? Does one of the huggers have both arms on the inside?* If so this gives them a control advantage over the other person. *What about someone walking down the street?* Their steps produce rhythm. This rhythm becomes predictable so you can calculate when they are off-balance. *What about choosing a seat in a restaurant?* Most experienced martial artists will fight (not literally) for the corner seat, so they have maximum visibility. This also means their most vulnerable location (their back) is against the wall and protected. Go to a bar with a BJJ black belt, steal the corner seat for yourself and watch them squirm as they are forced to sit with their back exposed to the rest of the room. It would be no exaggeration to say that training in martial arts changes everything about a person.

EGOS

Unfortunately, the holistic requirements of martial arts, paired with their competitive nature, can lead to quarrels between practitioners. Many clubs have signs above the entrance emblazoning *Leave your ego at the door*, which has led to this phrase becoming a clichéd expression in the arts. As foolish as it sounds, this overly competitive mentality became a real threat to the legitimacy of many arts in the past. People would attempt to smash bricks with their hands, feet, and heads, with varying rates of success – some still do. They would walk across fire to show they felt no pain. They would eat broken glass to demonstrate their internal strength and armour-plated sphincters. They would hang hundred-kilogramme weights from their scrotums (you read that right) tied in place by rope to show how tough their bollocks were. These things have been shown to be nothing more than party tricks nowadays, which hold almost no bearing on the quality of a martial artist – although I'm not sure I'd want to fight a man who voluntarily hung 100kg from his ballsack on the weekend. But things didn't end there. Showcasing physical superiority in the real world didn't prove enough for some; they wanted more. They wanted to instil the belief they could not bleed, be cut, or injured. That their bones were made of stone and their skin as tough as Kevlar. They showcased feats of magic, inhuman deeds, physically defying acts, and decreed they originated from pure bloodlines of ancient warriors dating back to the times of gods and demons. They aspired to show that their mastery of martial arts was unquestionable, that their training methods were superior, and that they, and only they, held the key to the most secret techniques with the most devastating power. They were just conmen at the end of the day, either after money, status, or a good ego stroking. But their involvement in martial arts gave the arts a bad name and created an image many are still trying to shun today. If you look enough (and you won't have to look that hard) you will find examples of so-called martial arts masters talking about *Dim Mak* (death touch), superhuman speed, forgotten pressure point techniques, and secret competitions they've won – but can't talk about.

You can make of it what you will but I'm calling bullshit.

It wasn't all bad, though, because their skulduggery helped shape mythological history, contributed to allegory, and gave many less gullible people a good belly laugh along the way. Their apparent superhuman feats were merely a product of the time, which could not be disproved as the ways of science had not yet been born. It's easy for us to laugh at these things now, but all those years ago when some peculiar looking bloke told you he could kill by just pointing at people whilst chomping on a glass sandwich, things were different.

As a point of comparison, early day sailors often proclaimed they had seen mermaids and sea monsters on voyages across the oceans, which now we know not to be true, but the stories still went down in history and helped shape the ideas and cultures of the sailor community. And we do not begrudge the sailors for these stories. If anything, we thank them for adding colour and mysticism to our history and culture. Well, one thousand years ago when some old Chinese guy proclaiming he could kick your ass by summoning the strength of a dragon before strutting across the surface of a misty lake into the distance is no different.

3

MYTHS AND PHILOSOPHY

*'Good judgement is the result of experience and experience the
result of bad judgment.'*

Mark Twain

MYTHS

Martial arts and mythology go hand-in-hand. This is obvious to see
in modern society. All you need to do is watch a few martial arts
films, *Crouching Tiger Hidden Dragon*, *Kung Fu Panda,* or *Ip Man*
to name a few. If you paid enough attention to these films you would
undoubtedly spot multiple, repeated, underlying themes: gravity
defying fight scenes, the old wise master, supernatural powers, the
antagonists and protagonists, and epic allegorical voyages. And this
would not prove coincidental. These universal themes are regularly
portrayed in many martial arts films because they are what the
myths and tales of yesteryear proffered. Yes, it is now known that
such feats are impossible, but this doesn't stop us from willingly
absorbing these stories for both their entertainment and
metaphorical teachings. After all, it's often said that fictional stories
can illustrate truths about the human condition that real life events
cannot scratch upon. Staying rooted in reality has its advantages, but
it limits our frame of reference and therefore stifles creative
progress.

The types of myths put forth were not just heavily
influenced by the people who created them (martial arts instructors,
monks, and religious personnel) and what their reasons for doing so
were (ego, status, protection, etc.) but by the societies from which

they sprouted. If we looked backwards, we would find that Asian and African cultures proved much more mystical and magical than European ones (at least around the times when the martial arts were saturating society) which is why many of the martial arts myths known today are derived from these locations.

When the origin of a martial art was unknown, or the head of a certain system wished to show how wonderfully charismatic they were whilst simultaneously bestowing their style with prestige, it was not uncommon for myths to be told about the purity and mystical powers of their art. Today, these stories are obviously fake, but it didn't stop certain people from propagating them in times gone by to showcase the apparent superiority of their art. Here is one such example:

> In a village oppressed by raiders, a group of Japanese farmers sent a young man in pursuit of help. After days of walking, he eventually reached a sacred valley where he fasted and meditated for 21 days. On the 21st day of his fast an immortal man appeared, known as Shorinjin, who granted the young man the art of Ninjutsu. Upon receiving mastery of the art, the young man headed for home. But on his journey back he was kidnapped by mountain demons who swept him away before swiftly delivering him to the King of Tungu. Taking pity upon the man, the King of Tengu bestowed upon him double-spinning Tengu swordsmanship. The young man then left the mountains and headed for home once again. When he returned to his village, he defeated its oppressors with the systems he had acquired; a system that has been passed down by the Saito family line to present.

Scrutinising the above is quite humorous. Firstly, if you were sent to fetch help, *why would you stop in a valley for a 21-day break?* Then, *why would you willingly starve yourself to the point of exhaustion when you knew your entire village's existence depended on you?* It's no wonder he saw an immortal man and mountain demons, he was obviously starving to death. And I'm certain that giving a starving man with very low blood sugar two swords and asking him to spin them in circles is a bad idea. But with joking aside, as I am satirically applying a logical assessment to an obviously fictional tale, such a story would have given significant kudos to the Saito family and their martial arts lineage. An intangible origin strongly appeals to the curiosity of human nature. The desire to discover what the immortal man and mountain demon's teachings were would undoubtedly have brought many prospective students forth, which in turn, would have increased the prestige of the school.

Other myths were formed to provide security to dojos and monasteries where martial arts were taught and trained. The idea of this was to deter martial artists of other styles from attempting an ambush. Martial arts schools were incredibly secretive in ancient Asia because the art's value lay in its techniques' effectiveness. Therefore, stopping rival schools from overrunning your dojo and stealing your wisdom was a very real concern of many. So, myths were created to minimise the chances of such a travesty occurring. You can see the same sort of information protection underway today, albeit not so much in the martial arts anymore. The militaries of many countries have information protection ranking systems. These systems rank the value of information by labelling it accordingly. An example of this information labelling is 'top secret', where only individuals deemed sufficiently trustworthy and in a position that requires them to know such things can access the information with this label. Other examples are 'open source' where anybody can see the information, or 'sensitive' or 'need to know'.

One such myth tells the story of a marauding band of Red Turban rebels who took it upon themselves to attack a nearby monastery. Upon reaching the monastery, their loud clumsy footsteps were overheard by a working kitchen porter. The porter immediately left his post to defend the monastery and was soon faced with the band of rebels. As the rebels began to attack, the porter transformed himself into a fierce guardian spirit named King Jinnaluo, who scared away the marauding band with a fire-stoking staff.

Given that stories such as this were believed to have been true, and that the spirits of guardians were known to be ferocious, the above tale would have undoubtedly acted as a sufficient deterrent to would be invaders. *Would you feel comfortable attacking a monastery that was purported to be guarded by a vicious, staff wielding spirit?* No thanks.

Yet other martial arts chose a different path for when it came to mythological propagation. They didn't conjure demons and spirits to defend their secrets, they aspired to possess the traits of power and invulnerability themselves. And they did this by perpetuating the idea that their martial ways made them more than mere mortals. One such example of this related to Ninjutsu, which is ironically famous for its secrecy. It was foretold that practitioners of Ninjutsu could snatch arrows from the air, mid-flight, rendering the bow and arrow futile. They could also catch the blade of a sword between their palms by moonlight and disappear into thin air without a trace. If the myths are to be believed (and they were at the time) they could even kill their enemies with a single empty-handed touch known as *Dim Mak*. The ninjas made themselves the stuff of nightmares – no gods, spirits, or demons required.

But even this wasn't enough for some. *If myths were to be told about your deadly efficiency, why ground them in quasi-reality? Why not allow the mind to venture into the supernatural and equip yourself with powers beyond the comprehension of uncreative mortals?* This is exactly what the Indonesian art of Pentjak Silat did. Practitioners of this art were rumoured to have indulged in the magical tradition of *Kebatian*, which orientated itself around a series of supernatural practices, chants, and trances. When studied studiously, Kebatian's esoteric techniques allowed its practitioners to harness the depths of dark magic that could be used to kill at a distance. The magic also offered protection to its followers, rendering them invulnerable. These same magical qualities could also be harnessed in other ways, such as fighting whilst in possession of sacred amulets, or hiding blessed stones and jewels in secret locations around your vicinity, which would provide you with power and protection in times of need. But martial matters were apparently not the only concern of students, given the power of such magic. Many were worried about their sex life. So, depending on the type of prayer you blessed your amulet with, and the time you spent praying with it in hand, the amulet could bestow upon its possessor, well, anything really, from fertility and intelligence to strong erections and desirability. And the more you prayed, the stronger the amulet became. But if someone other than yourself was to touch your amulet, even for a split second, its powers would diminish, and the amulet bearer would have to start from the beginning. Which, in some cases, meant the amulet owner would instantaneously lose their erection and have to pray to get it back.

In the art of Brazilian Capoeira, some students would practice something called *Candomble*, a religion based upon African beliefs, which if followed strictly would bequeath upon them supernatural powers, such as imperviousness to knives and bullets, and even the ability to transform themselves into animals and trees. *Imagine throwing a punch at someone before quickly recoiling in pain and realising you'd just punched a Douglas fir? How would you even start to defeat such a foe in combat?* Sure, this all sounds quite weird, but mythological tales often are. *If you believed your adversaries could morph into goats, chickens, cows, and trees (hopefully this technique will make its debut in the UFC sometime soon), where would you be safe?* A duck staring at you from a distance would make you more than uncomfortable. *If you held a secret discussion in the woods, how could you be sure none of the trees were your enemies? What about that Silver Birch? Was that there before? Why is it wearing a hat?* If such a story was

83

believed to have been true, undoubtedly it would quickly onset a state of paranoia about everything. *How could you ever feel safe if you knew your enemies could be anywhere and anything at any time?*

If we stepped over to continental Europe, we would find that martial arts myths also found their way into Greek mythology. It was said that Antaeus, the son of the sea god Poseidon and the Earth goddess Gaea, would challenge strangers passing through his territory to a bout of Wrestling. Yet no stranger could ever defeat Antaeus no matter how hard they tried. The reason for this was because each time Antaeus touched the Earth (his mother) his strength was renewed. So even when he was thrown to the ground he was invincible. This lasted until Hercules discovered the source of his strength, lifted him into the air, and crushed him to death.

As with the previous myths, we could speculate about what the above is trying to say. Perhaps it is saying that because Wrestling is such an innate art it was born from the gods. Maybe it's a symbolic attempt to explain that the Earth is the source of all power and should be respected. And that if you are weak then the Earth will selflessly replenish you. Perhaps its lessons are shallower than this and teach that overconfidence is a bad thing. Everyone has a weakness, and in time, it will be discovered.

That is the wonder and enigmatic nature of mythology. It's open to interpretation from multiple subjective minds, all of whom could be wrong, right, or most likely somewhere in between. But given the unbelievable occurrences that are present throughout most mythological tales, you would think these proclamations of superhuman abilities would have died a death many moons ago. But they have not. Even though science with its ability to extinguish ignorance is now an omnipresent feature within our societies, some martial arts practitioners still attempt to perpetuate superhuman ideologies and powers (with a straight face I must add) whilst claiming the science is wrong or has missed something. Many of these 'masters' have amassed large followings, or cults as they should really be called, and claim they can control their enemies' bodies (and sometimes even kill them) through the manipulation of *chi*, which is an energy present in air. There are plenty of videos on YouTube of supposed masters throwing their students through the air with the flick of a wrist or without even touching them. But fortunately for us, a chap named Xu Xiao has had enough of these fake masters and has gained somewhat of a reputation for challenging them to public fights (for some reason they accept) and showing them the true workings of real martial arts to a crowd. But still, even though Xu Xiao has won every contest he has ever entered, McDojos and fake masters continue to teach and push dangerous mythological beliefs onto their students. These supposed real feats are ridiculed within martial arts circles to such an extent that many martial artists of multiple styles have banded together (not always an easy task as martial artists can be famously tribalistic) in rebuttal of the bullshit. Satirical comedians have even latched onto the ridiculousness of the situation, such as Master Ken.

For the more acquired of mind, however, martial arts mythology has been viewed and used as a tool of historic investigation, not a means to exploit students and the vulnerable. The old stories have been seen as emblematic, some of which act as vessels of culture, and others that contain philosophical lessons requiring distillation. And this distillation process is where we shall venture next by posing the questions: *what exactly can the philosophy of martial arts teach us? And how did it shape the martial arts we see today?*

PHILOSOPHY

Philosophy in martial arts is everywhere. It's present in mythology, as we have just seen, literature, historical texts, cultural norms, societal caste systems, and can even be found in off-the-cuff remarks made by instructors or experienced students. And these philosophical teachings are responsible for the shape of the arts we see today. Sure, there are many variables that contribute to an art or individual's philosophical application, such as, *why is the individual studying the art (many people have varied reasons)? What is the current physical and mental condition of the student (are they fit, intelligent, strong, meek)? What was the art created for (warfare, everyday self-defence)? In which geographical location was it founded (existing cultural norms and philosophies would have influenced the shape an art would take)? In what period was the art's inception (different levels of technology and advancement can make a difference)? At what class level in society was the art devised (arts devised in poverty can differ from those founded in wealth)?* Plus, many more variables you can likely think of. However, as with training techniques and ensuring the mind, body, and spirit are factored into martial arts training, many philosophies overlap, with only a few exceptions that branch outwards on a unique stem into singularity. After all, if we whittle martial arts down to what they really are: defending oneself in a combative situation, then it is clear to see that many philosophies will ineluctably overlap, because all arts, even though they vary in their ways, roots, and origins, are focused on achieving a set, homogenised outcome: victory.

Morihei Ueshiba once said that 'if we overcome those enemies that attack us from within, we can attain a true victory over any attack from without.' It is clear to see that martial arts philosophy is concerned with two separate battles that are being simultaneously fought on different fronts. These are the battle with yourself, or from within, and the battle with your opponent. As with all things in life, it is impossible to succeed in the external if the internal is weak. And unfortunately for us, it is the internal battle that often proves the most difficult to win. To fully understand yourself, and keep those pesky internal demons at bay, it is important to know oneself in as much detail as possible. *What are your likes, dislikes, martial capabilities, and limits? Where lies the edge of your comfort zone? Are you willing to find that edge and make your comfort zone larger? How do you react in stressful situations? Are you mentally durable, decisive, and committed, or are you prone to faltering when push comes to shove? How much do you trust yourself?* The better you know the answers to these questions, the more likely you are to win the internal battle of self. And once you achieve this illusive victory, the external battles will become much easier. This shows that knowing yourself and how you can effectively apply your will in the real world is important to external victory, because 'you can only fight [in] the way you practice' (Miyamoto Musashi), and you can only practice within the parameters of the artificial limits you set in your mind. This is why when looking to succeed, 'everyone must choose one of two pains: the pain of discipline or the pain of regret' (Jim Rohn). Because without the required discipline in training, the only outcome is remorse, which is even more tender in its manifestation than the discomfort endured via commitment. Only discipline will allow a student to develop in the required way to ensure competency and success. 'When I go to bed at night, I'm a better martial artist than when I woke up this morning' says George St. Pierre, who evidently has chosen to suffer the pain of discipline. This makes it abundantly clear that negligence of self, in any form, bears no such fruit and is a one-way path to disappointment.

Yet as Soke Behzad Ahmadi once said, 'true martial arts [are] universal, simple and practical. Anything else is too complex to be used in combat', which is why focusing on oneself whilst choosing the pain of discipline over the pain of regret holds no prerequisite of complexity. True power is held in the mastery of the basics, because focusing on the foundations of an art is a tried and tested way to succeed. 'Take things as they are' states Bruce Lee, 'punch when you have to punch, kick when you have to kick.' If things are overthought, convoluted, and overcomplicated, then the chances of failure increase tenfold as it becomes easy to get lost along the way. And getting lost can result in defeat, which in the gym is fine and should be embraced by both student and instructor, but in real life defeat can prove fatal. This makes it evidently clear that a good gym is a place for experimentation and risk-taking and not a place for a win-at-all-costs mentality – this is what competitions are for.

The above presents the further, more philosophical question of 'what is defeat?' (Wendell Phillips) 'Nothing but education; nothing but the first step to something better.' Suffering losses is part of the natural learning process, so defeat in a controlled environment is nothing to worry about. In fact, it should be fully embraced as part of the journey. I would go as far to say that if you're a new martial artist and you're not being defeated you're either training at a terrible gym, or you're actively hiding away from risk and experimentation – both of which are devastating to progress. You should encourage yourself and your training partners to take risks in the gym because 'the more risks you take in the gym – the less you'll have to risk when it counts' (John Danaher). It's easy to slip into a familiar conservative groove where you feel safe, where you only call upon your favourite techniques and the people you face are predictable in their ways. The more risks you take in the gym the more your comfort zone will expand, and the larger your comfort zone the more dangerous a martial artist you will be. If you're a martial artist at present, you may recall that the first risk you took was walking into your current gym, most likely anxious about what you would experience and who you would encounter. But, without this risk you would not be training and improving in the way you are today. The same is true for the unfamiliar techniques and situations you encounter in the gym – embrace them with arms open wide. All the greatest martial artists are those who have taken the greatest risks. So, once again the adage proves itself true: no risk, no reward.

So how does philosophy state we should keep things simple whilst maintaining discipline and progress and striving to minimise defeat? Well, Koichi Tohei believed 'you should make a habit putting your all into every little thing you do', and if you do this, t culminated efforts of your day-to-day habits will reward you with success. Similarly, as was proffered by one of my ex-instructors about people who appear confused by a dedication to martial arts, and why someone may train each day: 'first they will ask you why you're doing it, then [once you achieve a good skill level] they will ask you how you did it'. The answer to how it was done is daily commitment (the exact thing they questioned in the first place) which is important '[because] fights are not won on drama. Fights are won on small, mundane details', says John Danaher. Details that can only be finetuned via regular, targeted training. And as we have seen already, this incremental method of progress is known as Kaizen philosophy. Simple daily steps that move you in the right direction at such a gradual pace that at first, they won't be seen, but as time passes, these incremental movements will compound making your progress visible to all and begging them to ask the question: *how on Earth did you do it?* They may then tie your successes to comforting ideas such as natural talent or good luck, but you will always know that no such thing is true, and that your success has been earned from the rigorous, continual application of Kaizen philosophy.

Once the discipline and rewards of training take hold, and the culmination of daily effort becomes apparent, it should become evident to students that clarity of mind is important to success, that 'the best fighter is never angry' (Lao Tzu) and that 'a quick temper will make a fool of you soon enough' (Bruce Lee). As we have seen already, even BJJ coach John Danaher agrees when he says, 'anger just makes people inefficient' and that 'no matter how stressful the situation you find yourself to be in, realise that success will come in the form of technical solutions, not appeals to our emotional side'. And I feel it would be safe to say that if Lao Tzu, Bruce Lee, and John Danaher can all agree on something within martial arts then it is most likely true. You see, anger can also lead to unpredictable responses and the faltering of timing and technique. Anger has a way of undoing years of training in an instant, so it is important to stay clear of mind in all situations. Therefore, 'do not let circumstances control you. [Given the correct training] you [can] change your circumstances [for the better].' (Jackie Chan).

Even if you keep your mind clear, commit to daily progress, and win the internal battels with your mind, it is still easy to become ensnared by the *martial* of martial arts. It's too easy to focus on the aggression, intensity, and combative aspects they present, whilst neglecting the lessons, philosophies, and morals they proffer. This is a very real threat to many practitioners of all styles, and it is important that one does not lose sight of the art's true meaning. Dan Inosanto appears to advocate this point as he states that 'the practice of a martial art should be a practice of love – for the preservation of life, for the preservation of body, and for the preservation of family and friends'. Even the movie icon Jackie Chan believes that 'martial arts [are] not for hurting people, [they are] for protecting people.' Therefore, it is through the harnessing and nurturing of love, understanding, and empathy that true progress will be made. And this is an important point that must be always kept in mind, because as a student of the arts, one is doomed to fail multiple times on multiple fronts. I would go as far to declare that success can only be found atop a mountain of failure, which is why it is by no means an exaggeration to claim that 'the master has failed more times than the beginner has ever tried' (Steven McCranie). This, unfortunately, is a painful truth. However, contrary to how it will feel on many occasions, mastery is not elusive and unobtainable; just keep on climbing. Use every fail as a steppingstone upwards. In the end, the more you fail, the higher you will climb. But mastery does not mean achieving a state of invulnerability, regardless of what the films and myths portray. There is always someone out there better than you, and you will also infrequently lose to people who are less skilled than you; such is the way of martial arts. So, it's important to understand that even for the experienced martial artist, 'martial arts [are] not about picking your fights and picking how things go; [they are] about adapting to how things are' (Gunnar Nelson), and 'you are going to have to suffer – over a long time. [In the martial arts] there really is no such thing as a free lunch' (Iain Armstrong). You cannot swindle your way into becoming a good martial artist – just as you can't in any artistic pursuit. Your work and ways are continually visible for all to see. Your skills, knowledge and capabilities are transparently challenged and showcased each time you step on the mats. But if you keep an open mind and strive to intelligently study the arts, it will become clear that 'a wise [person] can learn more from a foolish question than a fool can learn from a wise answer' (Bruce Lee). So, train hard, 'use only that which works, and take it from any place you can find it' (Bruce Lee). And once you have found it, hold onto it dearly and nurture it like a new-born child, because the idiosyncrasies of your art are 'like boiling water [which] if you do not heat constantly [they] will cool.' (Gichin Funakoshi). And maintaining this 'boil' is important, because when push comes to shove and your art must be applied for real, 'the fighter who gave their all [is the one who] will be around next year. [So] don't save anything. Give it all you got' (George Foreman).

Being a competent martial artist is a blessing because the arts have a unique way of improving character, confidence, morals, and perspective. But having such skill does come with a level of responsibility. This is because martial arts are not a tool to be used to instigate kafuffles, but a skill to be utilised in defending oneself in moments of need. This is why 'a punch should stay like a treasure in the sleeve [and] should not be used indiscriminately' (Chotoku Kyan). If this advice is not heeded, then this would show a lack of discipline and understanding by the student, or a paucity of quality tutelage from the instructor, for 'any martial art without proper training of the mind turns into beastly behaviour' (Shoshin Nagamine). Properly training within martial arts takes commitment, because they are a truly holistic endeavour, as we have seen, and their practices will seep into all corners of your life. 'I see martial arts as moving forms of meditation' says Joe Rogan, 'when you're sparring or drilling techniques, you can't think of anything else'. And this singular focus that martial arts offers to the dedicated student is 'one of the greatest gifts of the martial arts, [which can] ultimately guide us to new levels of spirituality' (Joseph Cardillo). But 'for me' proclaims Brandon Lee, 'the martial arts [are] a search for something inside. [They're] not just a physical discipline.' And if you desire to refine this inner self and learn the true lessons of martial arts 'you must live intensely, wholeheartedly, without reserve – as if you might die in the next instant' (Taisen Deshimaru). 'You need balance. That's why I like martial arts: it always tells you how to control your body, your mind, your heart' (Jet Li). So, it would be valid to state that 'the true science of martial arts means practicing them in such a way that they will be useful at any time, and to teach them in such a way that they will be useful in all things.' (Miyamoto Musashi). And if this is done, then the vessels of martial knowledge that have been handed to us from earlier generations can be further handed down to our children. And we should make a point of doing this respectfully, because it is true that 'the teaching of one virtuous person can influence many; that which has been learned well by one generation can be passed onto a hundred.' (Kano Jigoro). And if passed on successfully, then future generations will be able to continue in the indulgence and refinement of the arts, and eventually, 'see further than [we] ever did.' (John Danaher).

4

MARTIAL ART VS MARTIAL ART

'They called me short, I called them an ambulance.'

Karate Kyle

MARTIAL ARTS GO WORLDWIDE

As societies and technology progressed, it became ineluctable that martial arts would soon start to spread around the world. This was not a new occurrence, because as we have already seen, martial arts had moved from place to place before. Japanese Karate was influenced by Chinese Kung Fu; Chinese Kung Fu was born of Indian teachings; Brazilian Capoeira's philosophies originated in Angola; and Fencing was coined to have arisen in Spain before making the short overland trip to France. But this time it was different. This time, the globalisation of martial arts was achieved on a scale never seen before thanks to air travel, telecommunications, international trade, increases in peace and prosperity, and technological progress. The whole world was becoming more connected, more entangled, and martial arts were along for the ride. Military personnel from the USA brought Karate home after World War II; Kung Fu films saturated global entertainment resulting in a greater uptake of the art; books were written on the secrecies and enigmas of Ninjutsu; and the Filipino martial arts, on the back of foreign colonialisation, found their way to Spain.

As has been the case throughout history, when varied ideologies, philosophies, and beliefs clash, it often results in tension. Everybody believes they are right and the 'others' are wrong. The

93

masses tend to walk down the line of, *how could we be wrong?* Our techniques, applications, ideas, and beliefs have existed for hundreds if not thousands of years. So, if our ways were wrong, or there was room for improvement and development, surely someone would have noticed by now and the required changes would have been made. 'Our fighting techniques have been tried and tested in combat, so we know they're the best!' But the issue here is that everyone was thinking the same. Every cultural group had developed their martial art over hundreds or thousands of years. Each society had their martial arts handed down to them in ceremonial flair from the generations prior. All their arts had been tested against opponents to ensure their efficacy, so surely their art must have been superior. Everyone else was just misguided, confused, and wrong. Cultures believed with such intensity that their art was superior, they would bar students of different ethnicities from studying them. This is a situation that famously troubled Bruce Lee when he started to show the secret ways of Kung Fu to outsiders whilst his contemporaries tried to force him to stop. Schools would exist in secret, hidden underground or located in unmarked buildings and households. Students would be ushered in and out to ensure they were not seen. But it is clear to see why such mentalities existed at the time. A lot of martial arts had grown and flourished in tribal environments, whether that tribalism had manifested itself as village-to-village, family-to-family, or class-to class, the livelihoods of many in times gone by would have depended upon the exclusivity of martial knowledge, and the omittance of untrustworthy outsiders. But the thing was, even though this inward, closed mindset had proven valuable in the past, the game had now changed. Due to globalisation and an increased level of cooperation amongst individuals, true value was starting be found in the sharing of knowledge, and not in its withholding. But as would be expected, the open, free distribution of hundreds years of secretly acquired knowledge is not something you do or whim. So, it was held close to the chests of the owning cultures as if their lives still depended on it.

In hindsight, however, we can see this refusal to share martial knowledge and the belief of combative superiority is undermined by two factors. The first of which is a psychological cognition known as *availability bias*. In academic literature, availability bias is described as 'a cognitive bias in which you make a decision based on an example, information, or recent experience that is readily available to you, even though it may not be the best example to inform your decision.' This explains why each culture held the steadfast belief that their martial art was superior to all others. Each host culture had only been exposed to certain fighting ways, and those ways had proven effective in their home environment against known threats. Therefore, given the available information that the culture held (an in-depth understanding of their homeland and society and the combative ways of its people) it was obvious to them that their martial ways were indeed the best. But the martial arts were no longer operating in their home territory, meaning the environment and threats encountered were now different. In essence, the available information had changed, which could lead to alternative outcomes from what the cultures had previously experienced. In this new environment their martial art could prove *more* effective than it had previously, but it could equally prove *less* effective or perhaps even indifferent to the changes. Examples of the changes experienced would have been geographical, topographical, cultural laws and norms, and the social environment. All these changes would have had an impact on the efficacy of a martial art. This makes it clear to see that proclaiming the effectiveness of a martial art based on old or unreliable information is not just risky, but incorrect.

It was not just in the olden days that availability bias caused problems, however. It continues to do so today in all walks of life, not just martial arts. Many martial artists can become complacent in their ways because they assess their efficacy based only on readily available information. For example, a student of one martial art may be the most competent in their class and has been for quite some time. This could lead the student to believe that there are few better martial artists out there than them. After all, this is what their experiences have shown them, and each time they prove themselves superior to the other students in their class, this belief is reinforced. But, as we can see, the good student is not drawing their conclusion based upon all *applicable* information, they are doing so only based upon *available* information. And this is wherein the issue lies. Let's say there are 100 pieces of information required to form a full, accurate, unbiased conclusion as to whether this student is indeed the most competent martial artist. This is what we would call the *applicable* information, because all one hundred pieces are *applicable* to the equation's accuracy. But the student only factors in the information that is immediately *available* to them when they form their conclusion – let's say the *available* information is 25 of the 100 required pieces. This shows that the student's conclusion that they are the most competent martial artist is highly likely to be incorrect, as their conclusion is based upon only a quarter of all required information. Being the best in class is great, but the student may not know how they would respond in a real fight. They will likely not know how good the students of other schools and styles are either, nor how athletic or aggressive they can be. The student may also not know how their style matches up against other styles. These are a few examples of missing information that would be *applicable* to knowing if the student was indeed the best martial artist around.

Availability bias is not the only bias martial artists encounter. Many artists also fall prey to the equally dangerous *confirmation bias*. Confirmation bias often occurs when someone becomes sufficiently dogmatic about their beliefs. The most common example of confirmation bias is to be found within religion, where one religion may shun the beliefs of another because it does not confirm to what the individual holds to be unwaveringly true. This new, outside information may clash with what a person steadfastly holds to be correct, so is ignored in favour of other information that confirms and reinforces the person's existing beliefs. This same flaw can be found in martial arts. A martial artist may spend years studying a technique that is ineffective, and the longer they study it, the less likely they will be to question its true application. It's hard to accept that something you have spent years doing is ineffective and not fit for purpose. It takes a lot of courage to recognise and admit such a thing; but it's important to do. The martial artist in question may have seen the technique work numerous times in a controlled environment but has never seen it used nor been able to execute it in sparring. This is because the technique doesn't work against a live opponent and its application to real combat is purely theoretical. There are a lot of techniques in martial arts like this, which have been passed down from generation to generation based purely upon the fact that a figure of authority proclaimed it worked, even though robust evidence to the contrary showed it didn't. But after years of practicing and refining the technique, alongside being told by an abiding instructor of its efficacy, the information that points to the contrary of the martial artist's belief may be ignored. Excuses such as, 'I wasn't fast enough' or 'my timing was off' or 'maybe it was the wrong technique for that moment' will be made in an effort to maintain current beliefs.

As we can see, this approach causes many problems. It's easy to see how someone who started training in martial arts because they wanted to learn to defend themselves can spend their entire life learning absolute trash. But there is another issue hidden beneath the surface. Once you become convinced an ineffective technique or style works (due to the 'wise' profferings of an instructor or the sheer amount of time and money you have spent learning its ways) it becomes increasingly difficult to change your mind. And the longer you spend engrossed, and the more money and time you spend, the more difficult it becomes to escape. This leads to a person only selecting from the *available* information the pieces that *confirm* their existing beliefs, which narrows down the information pool significantly, meaning their beliefs and decisions are highly likely to be incorrect. For example, as we have just seen, to make a truly accurate conclusion we must factor in all *applicable* information. But due to the nature of our lives and how we cognitively function, we only have access to, and give an unbalanced preference to only that which is *available*. We saw earlier that this act alone can cause serious problems. Now, imagine only cherry-picking from the *available* information that which *confirms* your existing belief. As we saw above, the martial artist in question needs all 100 pieces of *applicable* information to draw the correct conclusion. From this, they only have access to 25 pieces, which is the *available* information. Now, let's imagine that only half of those 25 pieces of information *confirm* what the artist already thinks. This means that the martial artist is now establishing conclusions, creating opinions, and making decisions based upon only 12.5 of the 100 pieces of required information, meaning their chances of being correct are a miniscule 12.5%.

This shows us that not only are availability and confirmation biases prevalent and a problem in martial arts, but that confirmation bias fuels availability bias, and the more dogmatic you are about a thing, the stronger the confirmation bias becomes and the more likely you are to be incorrect.

This bias trap is exactly what the varied cultures fell into when they drew their conclusions that they were the best. They were simply (and innocently) acting upon and drawing conclusions from old and incomplete information.

The second factor is based upon a flaw contained within the belief; *our martial art is the best*. This is because this phrase focuses on a singular item (the martial art) which in turn presents the idea that it is only the art that matters in a fight. This is incorrect. There are in fact two elements that combine when it comes to ascertaining the quality of an applied art. These are the art itself and the artist. Both of which are required to operate in harmony if the true value of a martial art is to be seen. Therefore, it does not make sense to say *our martial art is the best*, and it makes much more sense to state *our martial art is the best when applied by the best martial artists.*

Let's break this down a little further to make it clearer.

Imagine that two individuals of different styles were to fight, both of whom had a mastery of their art, but one was superbly fit and strong and the other was out of shape. *If the fit and strong fighter won the contest, could it be said that it was due to their art being superior, or would their victory most likely be accredited to their greater physical conditioning?* I would say that their conditioning would have played a significant role, and even if the win wasn't completely due to their superior conditioning, it is highly likely that it still would have played a part. So, it could only really be said that *our martial art is the best* if the only difference between the two fighters was their art, and all else was equal.

We can play devil's advocate here and say that the physical differences between the opponents were due to their respective art's training methods, and this would be a valid point. *Would this then show that one of the arts was superior to the other?* Perhaps. But it also needs to be factored in that there are activities that can be undertaken outside the training hall that influence the effectiveness of a martial art. Things such as weight training, fitness training, dietary interventions, mental training, etc. *If an art leaves the physical development side to the student themselves and focuses solely on technicality and application, does this make it lesser of an art?* I would say no. So, in our hypothetical fight, the playing field is once again levelled, and the physical differences cannot be factored into the equation of *which art is best?* An individual's physical superiority does not then prove an art's superiority, but only the superiority of the artist themselves. A better way to prove an art's superiority is to have a weak, timid, small statured student beat a stronger, faster, larger opponent. This removes all physical aspects from the equation meaning victory is more likely to be due to the superiority of the art and not the artist. But even this approach has its flaws. Yes, fighting is predominantly a physical endeavour, but in many styles smaller opponents can beat bigger opponents due to non-physical advantages such as knowledge, experience, and cognitive speed, which takes us back to where we were at the beginning again. *Was it the art that caused the fight to be won or was it the artist?* Most likely it was a combination of both as they danced their inseparable dance. I would go as far to say it's not just impossible but completely pointless to try and answer the question *which art is best?* Sure, some arts are evidently more effective than others (we will encounter these later), but what all arts really want is an efficacious fighting system that is applied in combat by a physically impressive individual. That is the route to a higher rate of victory, although success is never guaranteed.

CULTURES MIX

This flawed argument with its availability biases and ill proposed statements continued to roar for many years. But this isn't to say all cultures kept their methods and techniques hidden. Some styles were more open than others. For example, the Japanese willingly taught Americans their ways (at least some Karate instructors did) which is contrary to what one may think due to the atrocities of World War II and the bombing of Hiroshima. Whereas on the flip side of the coin, the Chinese, and their myriad Kung Fu styles, were famously enigmatic. Kung Fu was, and still is, a national treasure and the Chinese appeared intent on keeping it that way. It didn't matter, though, that some cultures were more open than others because thanks to a greater level of globalisation the entwining cultures had begun and its progressive, unstoppable march was underway. This interlacing of all cultural aspects (food, drink, social norms, language, entertainment, and martial arts) would contin regardless of what the self-marginalised groups thought, which left them with a decision to make: join in or be left behind.

This was an exciting time to be a martial artist because suddenly, numerous previously unknown styles emerged from the woodwork, and people of contrasting cultures were presented with the possibility of exploring them. Americans and Europeans were soon able to study arts such as Karate, Kung Fu, Kali, Taekwondo, Hapkido, Ninjutsu, Muay Thai, and Kendo. Whereas Asians and other cultures suddenly had access to Savate, Fencing, Wrestling (Greco-Roman, Catch, Freestyle) and Western Boxing. But even though most schools did open their doors to foreigners, a stubborn few refused to partake in the cultural mixing pot, which on occasion led to feuds, fights, and inter-club violence. Even when I first started to study martial arts in 1999, some schools (thankfully not mine) still frowned upon training at different clubs or pursuing multiple styles simultaneously. In some cases, instructors simply didn't allow their students to pursue other arts and would banish them if they did. And if you wished to start training at a new club, some instructors would ask if you were training elsewhere, and if you were, they wouldn't let you through the door. Given the shape of the martial arts landscape today, it's odd to think that not so long ago this tribalistic mentality still existed. Obviously, we can only speculate as to why certain schools didn't wish to take part in this wonderful cultural amalgamation, but we can reasonably assume it was due to potential reasons such as a belief in cultural superiority (racism, fascism), a suspicion of outsiders, or perhaps the more benign reason of desired cultural preservation. Whatever the reasons were, as time went by (as we will see in the next chapter) if you fall behind, you are left behind.

Now cultures and martial arts styles were beginning to mix, this brought back the flawed question, *which art is best?* Schools would compete, demonstrations of skill and expertise were displayed, and instructors and students alike would boast of their art's dominance. All this boasting and self-proclaimed superiority

101

led many to investigate the ways of the arts to help ascertain what was bullshit and what really worked. *Did mimicking a praying mantis really prove effective in a fight? What about a dragon? Who had the most effective footwork? Who was fast? Who was slow? Did smashing bricks with your bare hands make you a tougher opponent or was it all showmanship? Were big, slow, powerful movements more effective than faster, less powerful ones? Was grappling superior to striking? Who was good with weapons? Which art was good at killing? Which was the easiest to learn? Was there even a best art?* Contrasting opinions also emerged such as the belief that sports fighting arts (Boxing, Wrestling) were better than non-sporting arts (Kali, Ninjutsu) as they could be tested more rigorously in fierce competition. Others thought the contrary, that the better arts were those that were too dangerous to be applied fully in training, which created the default belief that those arts must be superior because if they were used for real, people would be seriously injured or even killed in the training hall. One thing that did emerge was that the ways of many arts overlapped more than was originally expected. Sure, every art had its idiosyncrasies, but many of their basal movements proved almost ubiquitous. For example, if we isolate the technique of a round kick, we will find it is used in Karate, Kung Fu, Muay Thai, Savate, Silat, Taekwondo, Ninjutsu, Kickboxing, and Hapkido, to name just a few. Yes, there are variations on the kick's application and execution, but the kick is still a round kick. If we did the same for the grappling arts and isolated an arm bar (there are many ways to apply an arm bar, so we're focusing on any manifestation of the technique) it can be seen in Brazilian Jiu Jitsu, Judo, Japanese Jiu Jitsu, myriad Wrestling styles, Silat, Kung Fu, Ninjutsu, and Karate, plus more. This doesn't mean all styles are the same (not at all!) but it does show that at this time it was realised there were only a set number of ways of applying the human body in combat, meaning the secret to discovering which styles were better and which were worse didn't lie in the arts' basal movements, but in their intricacies, complexities, and philosophies. As with all things, the devil was in the detail.

An example of this detail can be found by comparing the differences between a rear round kick from Taekwondo and Muay Thai.

In Taekwondo, a rear round kick is thrown by facing your opponent square on and lifting the rear leg off the ground so that your knee is perpendicular to your opponent. Then, you would pivot your bottom foot so that the inside of your bottom foot is parallel to your target. From there, you would kick to your target by extending your raised leg to their centreline at a 45-degree angle, before retracting your raised foot back to the floor.

In Muay Thai, you should first step slightly to the outside of your opponent's centreline (if this kick was being thrown with a rear right foot, then this would mean stepping slightly to the left with your lead leg). Whilst stepping to the outside of your opponent's centreline you would also point your foot outwards to stretch the hips open, which helps create the effect of stretching an elastic band before letting it go. The rear leg should then leave the floor and travel towards the target at an upward angle of 45 degrees. Once the leg is about to make contact with the target, the hip should be 'turned over' and the foot on the floor twisted away from the opponent causing the kicking leg's angle to arc, allowing it to make contact with the opponent at the top of a downward 45-degree line whilst powering through the target like a swung baseball bat. The idea here is that if the opponent was not there then the kicker would spin 360 degrees due to the kick's momentum and follow through.

There are evidently pros and cons to each variation on the technique. For example, the Taekwondo kick, as the knee is raised perpendicular to the opponent, is more difficult to interpret, as it makes the round kick look like a front kick or side kick as all three of these kick types have the same origin movement. This could prove useful when fighting another martial artist as it's deceitful, but to a non-martial artist this subtle deceit would be wasted as they would not have the knowledge to compute the movement. Whereas a round kick in Muay Thai is evidently a round kick from the moment it is thrown. However, due to the stepping slightly to the outside of your opponent's centreline and the kick travelling through the target as opposed to just to it, the Muay Thai round kick is often considered much more powerful. *Which is best?* Well, as we already know, that depends, as it's impossible to separate a technique from the individual executing it. So, an experienced martial artist throwing a Taekwondo round kick would be better than an inexperienced martial artist throwing a Muay Thai round kick, and vice versa. But, for the sake of our thought experiment, if we were to make all other variables in the equation equal, except for the kick itself, then in my humble opinion the Muay Thai round kick is better.

This relentless art vs art debate continued: Karate vs Kung Fu, Muay Thai vs Kickboxing, Japanese Jiu Jitsu vs Wing Chun, Ninjutsu vs Wrestling, Western Boxing vs Taekwondo, and so on. In many ways, these debates continue today amongst some members of the martial arts community as they hold moot discussions about the intricacies of each art. Most of the time these debates are nothing more than a little fun, but there are some people out there who take this discussion very seriously. But the more the arts were tested against one another the more it became clear that although some arts were better in certain areas than others, there was no overall reigning champion. This made it clear that the martial arts still had work to do. They were now a global phenomenon, in a new landscape, being practiced internationally by millions of people. And if martial arts were to flourish in this new environment, then the requirement was clear: they would have to evolve.

5

MARTIAL ARTS EVOLVE

'No wonder these people don't believe in evolution. It obviously hasn't worked in their favour.'

Jeri Smith-Ready

EVOLUTION

To understand how martial arts began to evolve, it is first important to look at the sociological aspects of hierarchy, and the evolution of hierarchies themselves. This way of looking at martial arts evolution will allow us to group most arts into one of two pools: those that opted to evolve, and those that did not.

Before we investigate this, there are two points that must be made. The first is that all hierarchies are based upon value. The second is that the existence of hierarchies is inevitable.

We can see that the first of these two points is true because as soon as we give value to something, such as effective footwork, it places it into a higher position than something we give no or less value to, such as poor physical conditioning; therefore, creating a hierarchy of value. Another example of this can be seen by the fact you are reading this book and not another. At some point you decided you would rather read this book than any other you had access to, placing it at the top of your 'book choice' hierarchy. Something about it (maybe it was the dashing author) made you feel this book would be the most worthwhile use of your free time. If we were to list everything that has value to our chosen martial art and rate it on a scale of one to ten, we would quickly realise that a rather complex and robust hierarchy would be formed. This ineluctable

105

formation would then prove our second point from above, the axiomatic existence of hierarchies. As soon as value is given to anything, a hierarchy is established, and the only way to completely dismantle the hierarchy is to negate the value of everything in existence, which as I'm sure you will agree is biologically impossible.

But what does this have to do with martial arts? Well, as we know, every art places value on different things, therefore, creating their own unique hierarchies of value. For example, BJJ places a lot of value on chokes and leg locks, but not much value on throwing a good right cross or elbow. Whereas Muay Thai gives value to a good right cross and elbow, but not much value to chokes and leg locks, therefore creating a completely different value hierarchy to that of BJJ. In isolation from one another, neither hierarchy is better than the other as they don't need to compete. This is the situation many martial arts found themselves in before they went global. Their hierarchies of value proved efficient and effective in their isolated home environments against known threats. But, as the arts began to encounter one another on the international playing field, either in physical combat or under theoretical scrutiny, their hierarchies of value began to clash. *How effective is a choke or leg lock if you cannot grab your opponent because their punches and elbows are too effective? How effective are punches and elbows if you can only throw one of them before your opponent grabs and chokes you?* This caused many martial arts to revaluate their hierarchies of value and conclude that if they wanted to survive as truly effective combative arts, they needed to evolve.

It would be apt to state at this point that the evolution of martial arts was by no means a new thing. Arts had been evolving since their inception. For example, Wing Chun evolved from a rebuttal of more physical forms of Kung Fu, and in turn, Jun Fan Gung Fu evolved from Wing Chun. Aikido evolved from Japanese Jiu Jitsu, as did Judo, and from the roots of Judo, Brazilian Jiu Jitsu was formed. It is also known that Kickboxing evolved from Karate and as we have seen, Karate's evolution was influenced by Kung Fu. Taekwondo evolved from other Korean arts such as Taekkyeon, Gwonbeop, and Subak; and Catch Wrestling evolved from English Wrestling, before later giving birth to Freestyle Wrestling. So, evolution within martial arts was by no means unfounded, nor unusual. The difference on this occasion was that as opposed to a single (or small group) of arts influencing one another, this time there was an eclectic mix of arts from across the globe all coming together at once, publicly showcasing their strengths and weaknesses, and causing problems for one another they had never encountered before.

At this point, the arts were not in a position of unavoidable Darwinian evolution. Their evolution, or lack of, was a choice. In some instances, whole arts chose not to evolve, and in others, only certain schools of a given art embarked on the evolutionary process. In a couple of cases, students from existing styles broke off in their own direction and created whole new arts. This makes the evolution of martial arts fragmented and incredibly difficult to trace, because there are myriad variables that either aided or hindered the arts' evolution such as, *what country was the art currently being practiced in?* For example, Muay Thai evolved a lot in the Netherlands although it's originally from Thailand. *What was the political and cultural inclination of the country at that time?* The USA was more open to martial arts (and therefore cultural) changes than China. *How much globalisation was being experienced in the country or continent at that time?* Overall, Europe was becoming more global faster than the majority of Asia, which led to varied rates of evolution of the same arts across the continents. This may sound convoluted, because it is, but we can effectively pool these evolutionary variables into two sociological groups to help us better understand what happened. We will call these groups: conservative and liberal. If most of the factors influencing an art's evolution led to either little, or no evolution, we will call the art predominantly conservative. If the factors led to a state of change and evolution, we would call the art primarily liberal.

This conservative or liberal classification is important for us to trace how the arts began to evolve, because within an established hierarchy (in our case a martial art) it is the conservative mindset that tends to thrive best. The reason for this is that a conservative mindset functions better within set boundaries and known parameters; they tend to drift less and can manage their affairs better due to being more singular minded. This can lead to martial artists who fully understand their art and can effectively apply it without distraction. On the contrary, the liberal mindset is more open, creative, and willing to change. In many instances, liberal mindsets actively seek change and new areas to explore due to their artistic nature, which can lead to martial artists who fully understand their art but can become fixated on its flaws and limitations whilst creatively sourcing hitherto unthought-of solutions. It is important to state here, however, that neither of these mindsets is better than the other, and the martial arts that evolved most effectively (as combative arts) contained a balance of both.

At this point the predominantly conservative arts, governing bodies, and instructors became stifled and fell behind. Many of these people and institutions held onto what Bruce Lee described as 'classical mess', as opposed to seeing their new international environment as an opportunity to become more refined and effective. They essentially lacked sufficient liberal perspective to efficiently evolve. Whereas the primarily liberal arts became too conceptual and hypothetical due to a lack of conservative input that would have tested their ways more rigorously and ensured their art's efficacy more robustly. Today, the arts that were mainly conservative are more akin to cultural vessels. They have in some ways lost their way as truly combative arts but are great examples of preserved historic tradition. The arts that were too liberal, however, are not much more than an artistic expression with minimal roots. Their willingness to quickly change has led to a loss of culture, and their lack of tested, realistic application has made them no more than an elaborate dance. But evolution is by no means a singular occurrence. Arts that are mainly conservative now may become more liberal in the future and evolve, and arts that are more liberal now may benefit from a greater conservative influence in the future. Only time will tell.

This leaves us with one classification of art we haven't yet mentioned: that which managed to harness a good balance of both conservatism and liberalism. These arts are the ones that succeeded in the evolutionary process and became the highly effective combative arts we know today (Muay Thai, Kickboxing, BJJ, Wrestling, Western Boxing, Judo, to name a few). But there were two further prerequisites to these arts' successes. The first was that the art must not have been so terrible to begin with that it held no chance of becoming a superior combative art – there are more of these than you would imagine. The second was that the art had been given the opportunity to leave its home country and compete for international prestige. This may sound obvious, but there are many arts out there that have not yet had the opportunity to show the world what they can do due to reasons such as geographical isolation or insufficient exposure; for example, Coreeda, Mau Rākau, Limalama (possibly the greatest sounding martial art of them all) and Bokator. So, as it can be seen, the arts that came out on top of this evolutionary process were not simply the ones that evolved in the best way (although this was part of it) they were the ones that were also most willing to change with the times or had proven themselves so effective in their current state that minimal evolution was required.

CONCEPTS

I'm sure we would all be in agreeance that an effective martial art that has proven itself in situations that matter is a great achievement.

But the evolutionary process was not yet complete – and still isn't for that matter. Sure, it's great to have a selection of reliable arts ranging from striking to grappling and everything in between, but this still didn't present us with a singular art that was good enough (when applied by a sufficient martial artist) to win most of the time against any other art. This would require a slight change of tact and a new philosophical outlook on combat. It would take an idea that broke down the walls and limitations of the arts, allowing them to be open, free, and changeable, as opposed to strict, limited, and constrained. An idea that saw maximum effectiveness in combat achieved not via the lens of a singular art, but through the medium of a concept.

'Using no way as way; having no limitation as limitation.' (Bruce Lee). That very phrase is the essence of a martial concept. I quote Bruce Lee here because he is considered the father of conceptual martial arts, so it seems fitting to have them defined in his own words. Bruce Lee labelled his own conceptual expression of martial arts as Jeet Kune Do (JKD), but he apparently did so begrudgingly. It has been claimed by many authors and historians that Bruce Lee did not want to give his concept a name because he thought that by doing so, the name itself would cause people to view the concept as a stationary, contained idea, as opposed to something fluid and forever evolving. And in essence, that concern is the exact difference between a martial art and a martial concept.

When asked about JKD, Bruce Lee explained that:

I have not invented a 'new style', composite, modified or otherwise that is set within distinct form as apart from 'this' method or 'that' method. On the contrary, I hope to free my followers from clinging to styles, patterns, or moulds. Remember that Jeet Kune Do is merely a name used, a mirror in which to see 'ourselves'. . . Jeet Kune Do is not an organised institution that one can be a member of. Either you understand or you don't, and that is *that. There is no mystery about my style. My movements are simple, direct, and non-classical. The extraordinary part of it lies in its simplicity. Every movement in Jeet Kune Do is being so of itself. There is nothing artificial about it. I always believe that the easy way is the right way. **Jeet Kune Do is simply the direct expression of one's feelings** with the minimum of movement and energy. The closer to the true way of Kung Fu, the less wastage of expression there is. Finally, **a Jeet Kune Do man who says Jeet Kune Do is exclusively Jeet Kune Do is simply not with it**. He is still hung up on his self-closing resistance, in this case anchored down to reactionary pattern, and naturally is still bound by another modified pattern and can move within its limits. He has not digested the simple fact that truth exists outside all moulds; pattern and awareness is never exclusive. **Again, let me remind you Jeet Kune Do is just a name used, a boat to get one across, and once across it is to be discarded and not to be carried on one's back.***

(Bold added by author)

A martial art is something you learn, and once learnt, you use its ways to defend yourself in times of need. Whilst studying the art you may encounter techniques, movements, ideas, or philosophies you don't like, but you still train and apply them because that is what your art is, it is what your art demands. Your commitment to, and expression of the art is dogmatic. You don't change, alter, or omit anything because that would not be true to the art. You allow yourself to remain confined by the limitations of your chosen art, even if evidence points to more effective, faster, efficient ways of doing those same things. You are in essence a loyalist. But this is not a bad thing. Committing to a singular art can make you a truly superb martial artist, and by doing so you will also be educated in the art's culture along the way. It just needs to be understood that

111

you may never become the most complete martial artist you can by studying only one art. But this doesn't mean that fully committing yourself to a single art is wrong – not at all! There is much to gain (combatively and culturally) from becoming a true expert in your chosen discipline.

A martial concept on the other hand is much more fluid, open, and free. Of course, you must study a martial art to begin with, but once you have and you've gained a sufficient level of skill allowing you to scrutinise the techniques, movements, and applications, you do so in a cutthroat manner. You may study multiple arts simultaneously, because only knowing to fight in a single plain is not realistic in combat. You need to know how to punch, kick, grapple, and use/defend yourself against weapons such as knives. But once learnt, you do not remain loyal to an art's ways. You look at it from the perspectives of a philosopher, physicist, engineer, and artist, and make changes to your expression of the art as and when seems necessary or beneficial. You apply the outlook of a philosopher so you can question the content of your art, its ideas, thoughts, and visions to see if they are maximally beneficial to you. A physicist's perspective is also needed so you can apply scientific scrutiny to your expression of your art. After all, the expression of a martial art is not really anything more than applied physics, so it would be foolish to ignore evidence that pointed to a more physically effective way of doing something. An engineer's mentality is also required so that the processes and mechanics of the art can be scrutinised. Your chosen arts may have harmoniously shown you that doing X, Y, and Z is the best way to punch someone with a rear cross, but if study and experience (or maybe even techniques and mechanics from an art you have not yet fully scrutinised) demonstrate that a better way to achieve the same result is A, B, and C, then don't be afraid to make the change. Lastly, you must not forget to be an artist. As we saw much earlier, martial arts contain two elements, the *martial* and the *art*. Therefore, the requirement to be an artist is self-evident. By applying the vision an artist to your ways you can question creatively with no fear of failure, you can combine thoughts and ideas that have hitherto never been associated, you can think multidimensionally about the arts and what they proffer. This is the beauty of a martial concept; you can be unique and original in your approach to martial arts because your expression is yours and yours alone. 'Absorb what is useful. Discard what is not. Add what is specifically your own.' (Bruce Lee).

6

MODERN DAY MARTIAL ARTS

'Actually, on the contrary, my MMA career has gotten in the way
of my weed-smoking.'

Nick Diaz

NO-HOLDS-BARRED AND MMA

Given the world is a safer, less hostile place than it was 4,000 years ago, the chances of being punched in the nose today are significantly lower than they used to be. The problem is, though, that if you do get punched in the snout today, there are 4,000 years of refinement behind it. This improvement in clouting people is wholly thanks to the evolutionary aspects we have just encountered. And as we have seen, this evolutionary mechanism has resulted in the two main classifications of martial arts we see today. The first of these are the arts that have evolved into, or proven themselves to be, effective, combative fighting styles on the world stage. The second are the arts that have shunned evolution and the pursuit of maximally effective combativeness in favour of ossifying their cultural roots and traditions. Unfortunately, given the endeavour of this book, it is at this moment we must cease contact with the latter in favour of the prior. Because our journey is not concerned with the cultural preservation of the arts, but with their evolution and application in modern society.

People have been fighting since bygone days in sporting no-holds-barred style contests, which are fighting bouts with very few to no rules. Arts such as Pankration (Greece) and Shǒubó (China) provide ample evidence of this, as each of these arts are

114

what would be called a *complete* fighting system, meaning they train and fight in all zones: kicking, punching, trapping, clinching, throwing, joint locks, and grappling, as opposed to solely focusing on just one or maybe a few of these areas like certain styles of Karate and Kung Fu. You're probably thinking at this point that a complete fighting system sounds like a rather splendid idea, and you would be correct. This thought will then likely lead you into questioning, *how did non-complete fighting arts ever come into existence in the first place? Whose idea was that?* And the more you think about it the less it makes sense. It feels like somebody many years ago looked at fighting and said, 'Yeah, I see how it's all useful, but I just really like punching', and the incomplete arts were born.

Anyway, you will likely not be surprised to hear that the most well-known variation of this style of fighting we have today is Mixed Martial Arts (MMA). Modern MMA is not strictly a no-holds-barred fighting style because it does have rules in place to stop things getting out of hand. For instance, you cannot kick to the groin or poke in the eye; you cannot kick or knee a kneeling opponent in the head; no headbutts are allowed; no striking the spine or the back of the head; no throat strikes of any kind are permitted and you cannot grab the trachea; no hair pulling; no small joint manipulation such as the fingers; no placing fingers in orifices(!); and if you've had enough, all you have to do is tap your opponent and the fight will stop. There is also one often overlooked but rather substantial difference between MMA and the old no-holds-barred arts that are frequently (and incorrectly I should add) referred to as 'old MMA' or the 'original MMA'. And this is that the likes of Pankration and Shǒubó are arts, each of which sits within its own bubble, self-contained and restricted by its own limitations, whereas MMA is not an art but a concept. Sure, MMA is limited in some ways by the rules of the competition (it's a sport after all) but the techniques, methods, ideas, philosophies, applications, and concepts utilised can change all they want. If somebody wanted to enter an MMA competition and only use Wing Chun (good luck!) they would be more than welcome to do so. You see, MMA appears to be an art from an outside perspective because each fighter is employing pretty much the same techniques, which creates the illusion that they are using those techniques because they are what MMA demands. This is not true. Look at MMA 25 years ago and you will see a much larger variety of styles and techniques being applied. The reason there is an almost hegemonic method of fighting today is because much of the rubbish has been weeded out, and what is left are the techniques and methods that have shown themselves to be the most effective within this set sporting environment. This process of refinement is still underway, and I would confidently state that if you could somehow see what an MMA bout would look like 25 years from now, it would look at least slightly different than it does today. This proves the point in case. If MMA was a style (much like Boxing) then the difference between 25 years ago and now would be minimal. Sure, some Boxing techniques have evolved, and the conditioning of the fighters is better, but we don't see boxers throwing each other on the floor and suddenly choking each other unconscious because it's an effective way to win a fight. But, in MMA 25 years ago, many competitors chose not to fight on the ground because they either didn't know how or saw it as a waste of time. Changes such as this demonstrate that MMA is open to evolution and follows the conceptual path as opposed to that of an art.

This conceptual approach to combat has made MMA the fastest growing and second most popular combat sport on the planet.

THE EVOLUTION OF MMA

The beginnings of Mixed Martial Arts are very difficult to trace. But it would not be unreasonable to speculate that the combining of established fighting styles to form a personal, maximally effective combative philosophy, began eons ago in times less documented.

As we have already seen, some consider Pankration to be the beginning of MMA, which first appeared in 648BC, Greece. But for reasons already explained, I do not believe this to be the case. History shows us that Pankration is a *style* of fighting, similar to how MMA manifests itself today, but not a concept. And the true essence of MMA is that it is conceptual, open to evolution, and not confined by the parameters of an art – although it is constrained by the rules of the sport.

If you cast your mind back to the beginning of the book, you will remember we posed the question, *when did martial arts begin?* And we concluded this was impossible to answer. The same can be said for the question, *when did Mixed Martial Arts begin?* Or, *when did the first person or people start to approach martial arts conceptually?* Most of history shows us that even though arts have been crossing paths for centuries, which led to the challenging, borrowing, and combining of ideas, the result of this process was more arts, or variations of established arts; not a conceptual, adaptive approach to individual expression through combat. So, in order to answer these questions (or at least come as close as we can), we must focus on the evidence that exists, and not on what we can speculatively conject. It doesn't take much research to find a documented history of modern-day MMA, however. For if we leaf through the pages of history, we will find the foundations of modern-day MMA were laid in the boxing booths of Brazilian circuses during the 1920s under the term, Vale Tudo.

Vale Tudo performances started as style-versus-style bouts: Jiu Jitsu vs Wrestling, Muay Thai vs Kung Fu, Kickboxing vs BJJ. These fights would prove popular amongst circus goers, who gambled and chanted in unison whilst fighters of different arts went head-to-head in pursuit of victory. The Vale Tudo fights of this time had little to no rules, meaning bouts would often prove bloody and violent, much to the delight of the spectators. But although there were minimal rules to abide by, which meant combative expression could be explored, many fighters stuck fast to their training and chose not to adopt the effective techniques of other styles. This meant that although Vale Tudo was a great social experiment in the efficacy of various martial arts, which spurred change and reconsideration of what was considered combatively effective, it didn't fully bridge the gap between martial art and martial concept. The opportunity to do this was there, but the vast majority of fighters either chose to ignore it or didn't realise what was staring them in the face. This led to certain styles, namely Gracie Jiu Jitsu and Luta Livre, showing themselves to be some of the most effective arts utilised on the Vale Tudo circuit.

The success of Gracie Jiu Jitsu in Vale Tudo competitions led to the art acquiring a reasonable level of prestige. Due to this members of the Gracie family became certain that if they could carry their art from Brazil and onto the international stage it would prove itself supreme. GJJ had shown itself to be very effective against many other arts over the 50 years or so that Vale Tudo fight had been occurring. So, in the 1970s, Rorion Gracie emigrated to the United States of America in an effort to introduce Vale Tudo and Gracie Jiu Jitsu to the world.

Around ten years later, in 1985, Japan, similar ideas to Vale Tudo were emerging, and a fighting system known as Shooto was born. Shooto was the brainchild of professional wrestler, Satoru Sayama, who had trained in the Japanese art of Shoot Wrestling during the 1970s under the tutelage of Belgian-born German-American professional wrestler, Karl Gotch. This style of Wrestling was formed by mixing various arts such as Karate and Catch Wrestling, which helped produce a well-rounded, complete fighting system that focussed on all unarmed combative ranges. For four years Shooto proved itself to be an effective, calculated art. The combination of pre-existing striking and grappling arts showed itself to be a novel and effective interpretation of combative expression. But in 1989, things began to change. Shooto was struggling to remain self-contained, as the influence of other arts such as Kickboxing, Judo, Muay Thai, and Sambo loomed. This led to Shooto self-reflecting and questioning its interpretation of combat. As the pressure from external arts mounted, Shooto greater questioned its ways. *Was Shooto as good as it could be? Could it be improved by adopting external techniques from currently unincorporated styles? What was Shooto's philosophy and what direction did the art want to move in?* Then, in 1989, Shooto made the decision to bridge the gap between martial art and martial concept, by boldly transitioning from contained fighting system to Mixed Martial Arts promotion. Little was it known at the time, but this decision acted as one of the first steps of seismic change in how the world would view martial arts. This change enticed many competitive martial artists from across the globe to flock to Japan and compete, such as Erik Paulson and Jake Shields, which further caused ears to prick and heads to turn. Outside the martial arts community, this change in combative interpretation went by unheard, but to those in the correct circles, with their ears to the ground, it appeared evident that something was stirring, and change was on the horizon.

This change, albeit the first of its kind, remained almost completely isolated to Japan. This was because the promotion was only a few years old, so had not yet grown sufficiently successful to leave its homeland, cross the oceans, and make itself well-known internationally. But it only took four more years before the stirring of Mixed Martial Arts began to brew in the west, and the clashing of arts would begin. But unlike Shooto, the west's discovering of Mixed Martial Arts proved to have more vein beginnings, for it was not born of natural evolution, nor the selfless pursuit of martial improvement, but from a commercial attempt to prove that Gracie Jiu Jitsu was the greatest martial art of them all.

On 12 November 1993 in Denver, Colorado, a Sumo wrestler had his teeth knocked out by a Savate fighter after being kicked in the face whilst on his knees. A kickboxer fought a Karate fighter, which

119

ironically ended up a stand-up grappling match that represented two children fighting more than two high-level martial artists competing. GJJ was pitched against Boxing and won almost immediately when the boxer tapped out due to the uncomfortable unfamiliarity of mount pressure. This outcome is then repeated when Shootfighting quickly dominated Taekwondo, winning by heelhook submission. Next, GJJ is paired off against Savate, and wins by rear naked choke after circa 20 seconds of grappling. The GJJ fighter leapt in and grabbed the legs of the Savate fighter rendering his style useless by quelling many years of striking training almost instantaneously. Lastly, GJJ and Shootfighting pair off in the final. After an explosive start the fight quickly ends up on the ground. Both fighters exchange strikes before the GJJ fighter takes his opponent's back and forces him to tap from what looks like a mispositioned rear naked choke. However, although none of these fights would be considered spectacular by today's standards, they did change the way the world viewed martial arts. More to the point, and most importantly, they also changed the way martial artists viewed martial arts. The reason the fights were not so spectacular was because the Ultimate Fighting Championship (UFC) 1 was the first of its kind, which pitched many fighters from numerous styles against one another in a new, unregulated, unfamiliar competitive territory. Although this was the same format seen in the Vale Tudo fights in Brazil years earlier, this was the first time these types of fights had been broadcasted so widely and generated so much attention. In the west, before the UFC, martial artists had always fought other martial artists of the same style, competing within a format that was specifically established for the benefit of said martial art. However, the UFC was different. There were no rules, no time limits, and no emphasis on only fighting other artists from the same style. After all, as we know already, martial arts were no longer isolated fighting methods but global combative systems; and people were eager to know which was 'best'. After UFC1 was over there was little doubt when this question was hubristically answered.

The UFC had shown that size was not everything, and that a small, slender GJJ fighter known as Royce Gracie could defeat opponents larger, stronger, and more aggressive than him. In the minds of many in 1993, the greatest martial art on the planet was Gracie Jiu Jitsu.

It's a curious thought that GJJ, which had recently evolved from Judo and Japanese Jiu Jitsu, would in turn be responsible for the next stage of evolution in martial arts. In fact, after the initial handful of UFC events, the world of martial arts began to evolve at a rate hitherto unknown. At first, when fighters walked out to the cage, the UFC used to name their style on the screen so you could see which style was fighting which. Many of the early UFCs emblazoned headings such as *Ninjutsu vs Karate*, *Wrestling vs Taekwondo*, *Boxing vs Muay Thai,* and *Kung Fu vs Judo*. This was the draw of the competitions at that time. They were an extravaganza that aimed to determine which martial art was supreme. But then, without warning, the landscape began to change. This change could be attributed to the overlapping of three previously separate ideas. The first idea was born from GJJ, which at the time, after its success in Vale Tudo, unequivocally believed it was the best martial art on the planet. As we have seen already, the flaw in this belief is that a singular art could be considered the *best* way to fight in all instances. But, nonetheless, this belief spurred other arts to step forward, compete, and show what they were truly worth. The second idea belonged to the UFC, which took this belief of the *best* art and made a sporting competition based upon it – curiously, the UFC was initially founded by many including the world famous GJJ practitioner, Rorion Gracie, who had travelled to the USA circa 20 years earlier to prove GJJ was the best art in the world. By making the flawed *which art is best?* question into a funded, global spectacle, attention was drawn to the question on a greater scale than previously imagined possible. The last idea belonged to Bruce Lee and his Jeet Kune Do philosophy, where he stated that by limiting yourself to a singular art you are stifling your potential, and that it is better to adopt a conceptual approach to martial arts as opposed to dogmatically following a given art. 'Using no way as way, having no limitation as limitation.' (Bruce Lee). This philosophical approach primed the ground for rapid, effective, cutthroat evolution, where techniques, movements, and philosophies from various arts were both adopted and disbanded in the name of martial efficacy.

The combination of the above three ideas contributed to the concept of MMA that we know today. And, in an ironic twist, by attempting to pursue supremacy within the UFC, GJJ helped to knock itself off the top spot as the 'best' way to fight and became subservient to the concept of MMA. Don't get me wrong, GJJ is still considered an incredibly effective fighting method. But due to it being a singular art as opposed to a concept, it is stifled by its own boundaries.

The first notes of evolution and the birth of MMA came when Muay Thai and Kickboxing began to challenge the hegemony of GJJ. After the success of GJJ in the UFC, almost all competitive fighters pounced upon the art and began to study its enchanting ways. This, as you would imagine, started to level the grappling playing field. One of GJJ's main strengths in the first UFC lay in its ambiguity and mystique. At first, many fighters didn't know what GJJ was, nor how its techniques worked, which led to GJJ easily obliterating its grappling-ignorant opponents. But as the playing field levelled and grappling knowledge became more widespread, the efficacy of GJJ declined. This makes it clear to see that there is power in unique knowledge, and advantages to be had from keeping such knowledge to yourself. But once the ways of GJJ had been learnt it became evident that the best fighters were no longer those with just in-depth ground fighting knowledge, but the ones with both this and superior striking knowledge. Fighters were no longer so easily thrown to the floor and choked because they knew how to defend and grapple. The strikers had evolved. But in their artificially protective bubble of grappling supremacy the grapplers had been left behind. It was at this point that the grapplers began playing catchup and started to study the striking arts. *What good is grappling if your opponent can stifle your attempts, keep the fight on its feet, and punch and kick you whilst doing so?* So, just as the strikers had done, the grapplers adopted the conceptual approach to martial arts and began to improve their arsenal by studying striking.

This combative refinement process continued unabashed. Now the playing field had been levelled between the strikers and grapplers, fighters began to look elsewhere for advantages; and amidst that pursuit, *ground and pound* was born. Fighters had always punched, kneed, and elbowed each other whilst on the ground, but hitherto it had been more of a random, haphazard occurrence than a refined, calculated process. Hence the newfound obsession with ground and pound. Fighters began to analyse the 'striking whilst on the ground' game. *What was the best way to strike from a mounted position? What about when you're lying on your back with your opponent in your guard?* These questions were scrutinised, refined, trialed and errored, then scrutinised again until a strong, effective ground striking game was developed. Fighters became so efficient at ground and pound that sayings such as, 'You can turn a Jiu Jitsu black belt into a Jiu Jitsu white belt simply by punching them' became clichéd. Dogmatic followers of the striking arts used phrases such as this to fuel their pre-established belief that the striking arts were superior to the grappling arts. This is often the case when you are so invested in a system (not just a martial arts system); you lean towards the information that reinforces your established beliefs and shy away from that which challenges them, regardless of the quantity and quality of available evidence. And as the highly conservative strikers held fast to these misguided phrases as proof of their cause, the MMA community embraced the evident utility of ground and pound to their significant advantage. As you can see, the introduction of ground and pound made the MMA game more complex, therefore forcing the hierarchy of technical knowledge and expertise to change. No longer was it good enough to just know how to grapple and strike on your feet, you also needed to know how to strike (and defend those strikes) whilst on the ground. A simple reviewing of the UFC archives shows exactly what happened to the fighters who did not embrace this change.

Other methods of evolution occurred around this point, too, such as *sprawl and brawl*, which could be considered a defensive first, offensive second technique. A sprawl and brawl works by first stifling your opponent's take down attempt with a technique known as a *sprawl*, where you throw your legs backwards and away from your opponent's arms whilst dropping your weight onto them. Then you force the fight back to its feet and continue to strike, much to your opponent's annoyance. This technique significantly reduced takedown effectiveness, which gave strikers more of an advantage over grapplers, which as you can imagine, forced combatants who were predominantly grapplers to improve their striking game even more. It also led fighters to greater considering the application of their takedown techniques. Faints became more prevalent to help trick a fighter into succumbing to a takedown, as did the adoption of more varied takedown methods and the use of the cage itself. The MMA stance also started to evolve around these times when it was learnt that none of the existing martial arts stances suited the competition. Boxing and Muay Thai stances were too upright and prone to takedowns, whereas Wrestling and BJJ stances were too low and compressed to allow good striking and strike defence to be utilised. The entirety of the MMA game was being refined, and those who first found the solutions to MMA's problems became temporarily effective in the cage, until everyone else caught up.

This incremental refinement process continues today, with fighters looking everywhere for their next advantage. Over the years, fighters have tried training under different instructors focusing more on weight training, spent a greater amount of time conditioning themselves for the hardship of combat as opposed obsessing over technical perfection, mental training (a very interesting subject as explored in Alex Hutchinson's book, *Endur*

124

cupping, massage, studying lesser known martial arts in the hope of discovering something of value that is widely unknown, dietary refinement such as supplements, vegetarianism, veganism, and more. And the longer and more intensely this insatiable pursuit of martial refinement continues, the closer we come to achieving a state of martial hegemony. We are significantly closer to this today than we were 30 years ago, which is incredible when you think about it. Martial arts have been around for thousands of years, yet in the last 30 they have evolved and improved more than at any other point in human history. Yes, we have been building on pre-existing knowledge, of course, but the past three decades have shown us that a harmonised global pursuit of a singular goal is something worth aspiring to. In fact, it could be said that we have developed to such an extent that all the easy wins have apparently been made. No longer does a superior knowledge of grappling guarantee victory, as the sport of MMA is now much more comprehensive than just grappling vs striking. The big obvious advantages have been quelled via knowledge sharing and evolution; it's the small details that appear to make the difference now. Things such as learning to monopolise on the small holes in an opponent's game or studying their fighting style in detail and altering yours to effectively counter it. Saying this, however, there is actually still one significant advantage to be had by some, but it's completely outside of their control: genetics. As martial hegemony arrives and the most efficient way to fight becomes well-known, the greatest advantages (or disadvantages) will lie in a person's genetic makeup. As time passes, victories will more frequently be attributed to inherited speed, strength, suppleness, toughness, body shape, and limb length. It seems unfair to someone like me with short legs and a big head (I paint a beautiful picture of myself) that someone genetically longer limbed and more flexible would always have an inherent advantage over me if we trained equally. But such is life. I'm good at other things like sitting here thinking, for whatever that's worth.

It's at this point in time that a general consensus emerged on what combination of arts help create a good mixed martial artist, and this appears to be a blend of Boxing, Muay Thai, Wrestling, and Brazilian Jiu Jitsu. As stated, this is only a general consensus, not the rule, as other arts have successfully made their way into the sport and proven themselves very effective, such as Judo, Kickboxing, and Karate, to name just a few. But as a rule of thumb, the above styles have shown themselves to be supremely effective. Boxing is mainly used for its punching and footwork, Muay Thai for its clinching, kicks, knees and elbows, Wrestling for its takedowns, pins, and control, and BJJ for its leverage and submissions. Obviously, the quantity of each art within a fighter's arsenal will vary depending on the fighter's preference, but for pretty much all fighters these arts will be present in some way. Clyde Gentry III's book, *No Holds Barred: The Complete History of Mixed Martial Arts in America* is a great book if you wish to explore MMA in greater detail.

Nowadays, the next generation of fighters no longer need to undergo this 'studying multiple styles and trying to keep up with the competition' phase, because they have been raised on MMA from day one. This has its evident advantages, such as not viewing striking and grappling as polarised differences but all part of a singular, harmonious combative expression, and being able to reap the benefits of prior knowledge such as what techniques have shown themselves to be useless and what have proven themselves invaluable. But there are also downsides to growing up in an MMA bubble, such as reduced exposure to external arts, and learning to fight purely within a sporting context that has set timings for rounds and rules that incentivise things that may not be of most value in real combat. However, as with all things there is always a compromise to be made, and I personally feel that MMA manages this compromise well and is one of the best ways to learn to fight on the planet. But we must still remember that MMA is a sporting art, which in the eyes of some makes it not a true martial art. MMA has also become so obsessed with martial effectiveness that it can sometimes relegate the *art* in a singular minded, fanatical pursuit of the *martial*, which as we have already seen can hold consequences for the artist in the long run. *Is the pursuit of martial arts purely a physical endeavour, or should there be a mental and spiritual aspect to them also?* Well, you have already read my opinion on this in earlier pages. I believe the commercialisation of martial arts is a double-edged sword. On one side, global access to martial arts is a fantastic thing. It allows the arts to improve the lives of millions, gives many the skills required to defend themselves and their families, brings more minds to the table which means more ideas, more trial and error, and more improvement. If it were not for the commercialisation of the arts we would not be where we are today, and we would not have seen the astounding progress we have witnessed over the past 30 years, which would be a real shame. But the other edge of the sword shows us that too aggressive a commercialisation of martial arts can lead to a dismissal of the artistic side. It can force arts to conform to global pressures and politics. It can take the arts from their original martial form and change them into sporting styles that are less comprehensive and less complete, less fulfilling, and less beautiful. This, in turn, causes techniques and methods to be forgotten and forces them to evolve in a purely sporting context as opposed to evolving from real combative situations. If pushed too far, this process can strip a martial art of its soul entirely and transform it into nothing more than a cardiovascular workout sold to gymgoers as the latest fitness trend. Now, that is a tragedy to bemoan.

What I have expressed is not an original thought by any means, as it was exclaimed many years ago by Miyamoto Musashi in *The Book of Five Rings* when he said, 'As I see society, people make the arts into commercial products; they think of themselves as commodities, and also make implements as items of commerce. Distinguishing the superficial and the substantial, I find this attitude has less reality than decoration. The field of martial arts is particularly rife with flamboyant showmanship, with commercial popularisation and profiteering on the part of both those who teach the science and those who study it.' As I have very recently mentioned, the answer to this complex situation is balance and compromise. Complete committal to globalisation and commercialisation will dilute and dissolve the arts, whereas not showcasing or spreading an art outward can lead to stagnation, inefficacy, and even extinction. It's a precarious tightrope to walk, but walking it successfully is integral if we wish to preserve the true essence of martial arts for future generations.

SCIENCE

Possibly the most obvious and important question in martial arts we have not yet asked is, *do they work? Is it worth spending years of your life training in martial arts to learn how to adequately defend yourself? Or is it all just rubbish?* These are incredibly important questions that deserve an answer, and lucky for us the answer is short and simple: yes, they work. Obviously, studying martial arts is not a guaranteed road to combative success, but they will significantly increase your chances. You could be a confident, highly skilled martial artist but still be defeated in the street by another, more highly skilled martial artist. You could also be defeated by a weapon such as a knife or gun, or a group of people who attack you as an individual, or even a lucky punch that catches you off guard from a non-trained fighter. There are many ways in which an experienced martial artist can be defeated in a fight, but as mentioned, the martial arts offer no such guarantee of victory, simply an advantage over a lesser skilled opponent.

The truth of martial arts effectiveness can be found in other ways. If martial arts were ineffective then people walking off the street would enter gyms and have a statistically even chance of beating up those who have been training for years, which would showcase the inefficacy of the arts and cause a mass exodus of students. But this has not happened. Random people would be entering and winning Boxing, Judo, BJJ, Sambo, Muay Thai, Kickboxing, and MMA competitions with no training, which has also not happened. Things such as the famous 'Gracie Challenge' where any person (martial artist or otherwise) could challenge the Gracie family (one of the founding families of modern day BJJ) to a fight would have fallen flat on its face when it was realised that victory was statistically down to luck and not skill. At present, a caricature has emerged of an individual who proclaims that 'martial arts don't work on me' and that 'when I get angry, I see red, and bodies hit the floor'. This shows incomprehensible ignorance towards the effectiveness of martial arts and the ways in which they have proven themselves over the years. I, and I will not be alone here, have walked into many martial arts clubs over the years and continually found myself at a rather sizeable combative disadvantage. This, from my own empirical experience, has shown me on many occasions the sheer devastating potency of martial arts. Thousands of years of trial, error, experimentation, and risk have indeed allowed us to refine the art of using our bodies as a weapon. And the results are addictive.

So, now we have established that the martial arts *are* effective, let's look at exactly *how* effective they are. I will not be investigating historical events to address this point such as the use of Capoeira against the Dutch, the application of Kali in the Philippines against Spanish invaders, or the use of Jiu Jitsu and Kendo by the Samurai to control and suppress underlings. The effectiveness of martial arts is clear to see today via their application in competition and military skirmishes. But I wish to see *what* the arts are capable of when measured. We all know that a Muay Thai kick is effective, *but how effective is it? How hard can it hit you?* We also know that trained martial artists are fast, *but how fast?* The grappling arts are expert at joint manipulation, *but what exactly are they capable of if applied fully in combat? What can the body achieve when pushed to the known limit?* These are great questions, and luckily for us, a TV show named *Fight Science* has given us some insight.

HOW HARD CAN YOU PUNCH?

Let's first look at one of the most delightful experiences – being punched in the head. *How much impact do you think your skull can take? How hard do you have to be hit in the head for your skull to fracture?* The skull is one of the most fragile parts of the human body, and contained inside around half of all people's skulls is something called a brain. Given the brain is the seat of consciousness and the power centre of the body, it would be reasonable to say it's probably worth keeping safe. Hence the rather solid bony ball that sits atop your neck that you're currently looking out of. But as with all things, no matter how brilliantly evolved the skull may be, it has its weak spots. Namely, the temples. If you trace your fingers from the outside of your eyes to the top of your ears, your temples are located about one-third of the way along that line. You can feel where they are if you trace the line with a reasonable amount of pressure as they feel softer and more squidgy than the rest of your head. The temples are a latch where four skull bones fuse, making it more vulnerable to pressure than the rest of the head and more likely to become damaged if hit. *So, how much pressure would it take to fracture the skull at the temples?* Well, the answer to this will obviously vary per individual, but as a ballpark figure, would be safe to say circa 1,100lbs (500kg) of force. I think this a rather reassuring number, which gives me faith in the durability of my head. But here is wherein the problem lies. A group of researchers undertook an experiment where they looked to quantify the force of a boxer's right cross – a rear hand straight punch. The boxer was not selected because he was the most famous boxer in the world, nor because he was known for his particularly powerful punches. He was most likely selected because he was available on the day of shooting and was interested in seeing how hard he could punch, which is not the most rigorous of qualifying criteria. Regardless, he wrapped his hands, took his stance, and threw his right hand as hard as he could towards the pressure pad. Once the punch had been analysed and the data recorded, it was revealed that the punch had struck the pad with 1,000lbs (454kg) of force. A mere 46kg short of the force required to fracture the average skull. This is quite astounding when you think about it, as a non-trained fighter would struggle to generate half this force. But via the pursuit of Boxing, average people have become so powerful with their hands that they are a cat's whisker from fracturing your skull with a single punch. But there's more. The famous Vale Tudo fighter Bas Rutten was also measured to see how powerfully he could deliver a right hook to the body of a humanoid dummy. Bas casually approached the dummy, positioned himself, and let the punch swing with everything he had. The dummy rattled like it had been hit by a car as the power of the punch reverberated throughout its entire body. The scientists who were measuring the punch exhaled in astonishment at the sheer force generated. It was obvious from the sound of impact that the punch was hard, and that none of the observers considered a career change to professional fighter or crash test dummy. Once the results were in, the scientists' impressions were confirmed via the dumbfounded looks on their faces. Bas had managed to conjure a jaw-dropping, stomach-aching, nerve-shredding 1,300lbs (590kg) of force in a single punch – enough to rupture the spleen and hospitalise an individual. This, to me, is an incredibly potent display of the effectiveness of martial arts. And a compelling reminder to never pick a fight with Bas Rutten.

But what do fighters do to generate such power? The answer lies within something known as kinetic linking. Most untrained boxers (or martial artists) will punch with the arm only, meaning most of the power of the punch is generated by the triceps and front deltoid. But punching in this way will generate very little power and cause almost no damage to your opponent. Boxers, on the other hand, have learnt to put their entire body (strength and weight) behind a punch. This is because for a boxer, a punch does not come from the arm, but from the feet. By driving the rear foot into the ground, a boxer takes the energy from this motion and carries it up throughout their body. This energy will pass through the thigh and into the hips, at which point the torso will be rotated to both continue the movement of the energy whilst adding to it with the muscles of the core. The energy will then continue to rise throughout the body and into the large muscles of the back and chest before entering the arm. Once in the arm, the deltoid and triceps are incorporated, allowing the arm to extend and the fist to strike through its target with considerable force. And the faster this chain of events occurs, the less energy that is lost between the driving of the foot and the striking of the fist. It's a supremely effective way of generating power, and the secret as to how a boxer can punch at a force equal to multiple times their own bodyweight.

HOW FAST CAN YOU STRIKE?

As we have just seen, through the use of kinetic linking and years of dedicated martial arts training, it's possible to punch with a rather intimidating 590kg of force – that's half the weight of a small car. *But how is it possible to produce so much power?* Well, as we saw, the effective utilisation of kinetic linking allows fantastic amounts of power to be employed. But, regardless of its efficacy, kinetic linking doesn't tell us *how* to produce power, it simply provides us with a *way* of doing so. *So, how is power produced?* Well, the answer is found in the very simple equation: speed + strength = power. This means that to attain the 590kg of force we saw Bas Rutten apply, there must be a solid foundation of speed and strength in place. This speed and strength can then be applied throughout the kinetic linking chain to maximise its effectiveness. The more speed and strength you possess, the more power you can generate and the more damage you can cause. So, given that speed is half the power equation, it's easy to see why every martial artist on the planet is obsessed with speed and harnessing as much of it as their physical potential allows. But speed is not just a means to producing power, as it comes with myriad other benefits such as the ability to outmanoeuvre, outpace, out-strike, and out-scramble your opponents. It's an integral vertebra in the backbone of effective martial arts.

This train of thought naturally leads us to the question, *how fast can a trained martial artist move?*

If we wish to accurately answer this question there are two factors we must consider, one of which is mental and the other physical. And both aspects are important if speed is to be effectively applied in combat. Mental speed relates to reaction time, whereas physical speed relates to the rate at which your muscles can accelerate. If a martial artist has muscles that can accelerate at a profound pace but cannot mentally react to being politely tossed a tennis ball, they would be truly useless in a fight, and probably in most of real life too. Although they would make a fun friend to throw objects at. On the flip side, if we had a martial artist whose mental reactions were lightning fast, but they were so physically slow they could barely move, they would also be useless in a combative situation. As an example, mid-fight, they would be completely aware of the size 10-foot heading inconveniently towards their groin. They would be able to taste the pain of impact before it occurred. They just wouldn't be able to do anything about it as their physical reactions were too slow.

So, as we can see, as always seems to be the case, a balance is needed. And the more of each type of speed someone possesses, the faster they are.

Fight Science decided they could accurately measure a martial artist's reaction speed by linking up a motion-capture high-speed camera alongside four red strike pads with accompanying

133

LED lights to mimic the movement of the limbs of a real opponent. The martial artist would also be wearing a movement tracking suit imbedded with laser lights and sensors that can record their movement at a rate of more than 2,000 measurements per second. The idea was that once a bulb positioned on a designated pad lit, the martial artist would strike that pad as quickly as they could. Sort of like a scientific whack-a-mole but without the moles, making it much less fun. This would allow the scientists to gauge the time between the bulb lighting up and the moment of impact on the strike pad. The shorter the period between the two meant the faster the mental and physical reaction times of the martial artist. The mental reaction time could be seen by measuring the time between the bulb lighting and the martial artist starting to move. This would show the time it had taken for the lit bulb to be computed, and the mind directing the body to move. The physical speed would be measured by calculating the time between the start of the movement and the moment of impact on the pad.

The average person takes around one fifth of a second to perceive a lit bulb. By this time, however, a trained martial artist has already recognised the bulb is lit, computed the information, decide how best to react, and started to move. Once the decision to react has been made, electric signals travel down nerve fibres in the body at nearly 225 miles per hour to activate the chosen muscles that will execute the strike. In this experiment it was found that the time between the LED bulb lighting and the hand striking the designated pad was a lightning-quick 0.18 seconds. Twice the speed at which a human eye can blink. Astonishingly, the average person takes 0.20 seconds to simply recognise a bulb is lit, meaning an average Joe would have been punched in the face 0.02 seconds before they realised anything was happening. This is highly valuable information. The 0.02 seconds may not sound like much, but it is the difference between hitting someone primed to defend themselves and striking someone who is completely unaware they

134

are in danger. Yes, the variance in timings is small, but the real-life difference when applied to a live combative situation is significant.

I once used to kickbox with a guy who was considerably better than me in all regards. He was stronger, more flexible, had better timing, a more thorough understanding of techniques and their application, and was considerably faster and more accurate than me. If you have never experienced such a thing, then I think it is difficult to understand the frustration of fighting someone who seems to compute and move on a much faster level than you. It's like fighting a ghost. His mental and physical speed was such that as soon as he saw me initiate a jab, he could kick me in the head before my lead hand reached him. To this day I have no idea how he moved so quickly. I was by no means slow (I was also by no means fast), but time after time he outmanoeuvred, outpaced, and outwitted me in what looked like an effortless dance. I used to try and justify my inadequate speed in other ways. Perhaps I was telegraphing moves. Maybe I was just not as fit as him, so I tired more easily. Perhaps my technique wasn't up to scratch. Whatever it was (I was most likely just slow – don't let me try and kid myself) those 0.02 seconds made it almost impossible to compete on the same level. For all I knew, the difference may as well have been ten minutes. The outcome would have been the same.

Via experimentation, it has also been seen that martial artists have the speed to strike (a clean, technically effective strike, not just flapping arms and legs around) at a rate of over 100 strikes per minute. Not only does this showcase good speed, but it also demonstrates strong muscular endurance to maintain such pace.

In a rather fun little test, a biomechanical engineer and sports physiologist wanted to see who was fastest: a martial artist or a snake. Specifically, a venomous albino western diamondback rattlesnake. Aptly, the martial art of choice was Wushu Kung Fu. As you will know from books and TV shows, when threatened, a snake coils its body like a spring. This enables the snake to launch forward with maximum speed and strike. As soon as the snake has struck its target, it recoils its body back to the spring-like formation, so it is poised and ready to attack again. Snakes are famous for their speed, so in this experiment a scaly diamondback seemed to be a worthwhile yardstick to measure us clumsy humans against.

The aggravated, highly venomous rattlesnake was given a red party balloon, which only seemed to annoy it further. The snake was then recorded using a high-speed camera so the speed of its party crashing, balloon popping strike could be measured. In a tense moment of silence, the onlookers knew it was only a matter of seconds before the party was over. The snake coiled, flicked out its tongue, and eyed the balloon like an old foe. Its tail began to rattle which only added to the party theme in honesty. After a moment's hesitation, the snake struck the red balloon causing a dramatic explosion. The high-speed recording was then scrutinised millisecond by millisecond. Some quick calculations were done and the results were in. The snake travelled 4.65 inches (11.81cm) in 29.5 milliseconds, which equates to a speed of 13.12 feet (4 meters) per second. The party was over. No snakes have been invited to birthdays since.

But what are us humans capable of with good training? When the Kung Fu fighter was given the results of the snake's strike and asked if they thought they could move faster, they humbly and elaborately replied, 'I'll try'. A life-size polyurethane head with bright blue eyes and a shining bald head was placed on a flexible spike, like a beheaded enemy of Vlad the Impaler. The martial artist was then given instructions to target the eyes when they strike, with the catch that the head would not remain stationary when they attempted to strike but would randomly move around on a robot arm like a 1980s Hollywood monster. This seemed a little unfair to me as the snake just had to hit a stationary balloon, but I suppose this bobbing head made for better TV. The Kung Fu fighter's finger was then marked with a dot to make it easier for the high-speed camera to track, and the head began to weave. The martial artist tracked the movement of the head, with their lead hand poised as ready to strike. The head, on its robotic arm, nightmarishly bobbed and ducked whilst always maintaining a creepy and prolonged eye contact. In the head's defence, it did have no eyelids, so I suppose it didn't have much choice. Unfazed, the martial artist peered back, focussed, poised. The head was moving surprisingly fast, but the Kung Fu fighter's hand smoothly traced its movements with only a partial delay. Then, once the moment presented itself, they struck. Impressively, the fingers of the martial artist struck perfectly into the eyes of the head in what looked like a rather painful finger poke. The camera is then played back, the distances and speed are noted, and the mathematics computed. The scientists and martial artist apprehensively stood around a table waiting for the result to be presented. A minute later, the results were in. The snake, now back in its box, must have looked deflated like the balloon it popped when it heard the human had struck at 4.2 meters per second – 0.2 meters per second faster than it did.

The snake and martial artist went their separate ways.

HOW POWERFULLY CAN YOU KICK?

Out of an NFL footballer, a Muay Thai fighter, a footballer (soccer), Capoeira fighter, a Karate fighter, and a Taekwondo fighter, who do you think has the most powerful kick?

It's a difficult question but take a moment to try and put them in order from what you think will be the least to the most powerful.

Before I researched this part of the book, I considered this question like you're doing now. It's a very difficult question to answer as there are many variables to consider, but the greater the knowledge you have on each of the listed disciplines, the easier I think you will find it to answer. So, before we see the results, I will give you my thoughts on this question to see if our methods of thinking overlap.

Firstly, I tried to consider the main variables. These numbers were found via experimentation on individuals. Motion sensors were strapped to limbs, impact pressure sensors were fastened to bags and balls, and high-speed cameras were used to track movements and technique. So, the first variable I needed to consider was *what type of kick would each person choose to throw?*

Each of the individuals measured was given free rein to choose whatever kicking technique they liked. This would obviously have a rather significant impact on the results of the experiment (and may even help shape your answer) and generated a lot of leeway for a poor choice of kick. But personal choice was encouraged, fair judgment given, and all decisions respected as they were made based on each person's expertise in their respective discipline.

Firstly, the NFL footballer chose a punt, where the ball is dropped out of the hands and then kicked up field before it hits the floor. I have almost no knowledge of NFL, but my initial thoughts were that this was a big kick. One of the few things I do know about NFL is that this kicking technique is used to kick the ball far up field, so it must have been a reasonably powerful kick and therefore a decent choice.

The Muay Thai fighter was next and he choice a round kick – no surprises there. This is a staple kick in Muay Thai that's so well known for its power it has become synonymous with the art. It's the kick I would have chosen if I were taking part in this experiment, so this gave me confidence the Muay Thai fighter would perform well.

After the Muay Thai fighter came the footballer. Being from the UK I obviously know football. I can't stand the game and have been trying to avoid it my entire adult life. But begrudgingly I understand it. The footballer chose to kick the ball from a penalty spot. This meant the ball sat stationary on the ground and the footballer ran up to it and kicked it. Given footballers fall over nothing, can be blown over by the wind, and cry when touched by light drizzle, I had no faith in any power in this kick, so disregarded it immediately.

Next up was the Capoeira fighter. Capoeira is one of those martial arts that many other martial artists know very little about. This made it difficult to judge the named kick which was sort of like a Muay Thai round kick, but it started from the floor. The name of the kick is Martelo de Negativa (possibly the coolest sounding kick in existence), but I thought it would achieve a middle of the road performance – how wrong I was!

After Capoeira came Karate. Karate is a hard, no-nonsense martial art that focuses on a solid, conditioned body that is capable of both giving and receiving intolerable punishment. This gave me faith that the Karate fighter would perform well, until the kick he chose was a front kick. I found this confusing because my years spent practicing martial arts had taught me there were many other kicks considered more powerful than the front kick. Sure, a front kick is fast, hard to stop, and incredibly effective, but it's not considered the most powerful of kicks. This led me to giving the Karate fighter a low estimation of kicking power.

Lastly, it was the turn of the Taekwondo fighter. This was an interesting and difficult proposition. I would say Taekwondo is the martial art most famous for its kicks and kicking speed. The hip mobility, hip flexor strength, and flexibility of Taekwondo fighters is something to be admired. I would not say, however, that Taekwondo is the art most famous for kicking power. The kick of choice was also surprisingly a round kick. This may not come as a surprise to many readers, but it did to me. I feel I could have predicted with 95% accuracy that the Muay Thai fighter would choose a round kick, but for some reason I expected the Taekwondo fighter to opt for a spinning sidekick or something similar. Either way, his decision was made, and the Taekwondo fighter selected the round kick.

The second variable I factored into my equation was biomechanical. In other words, *how did the participants move when they threw their kick? Did they move smoothly? How much bodyweight did it look like their kick contained? Did the movements appear to involve lots of different muscle groups or just one? Were the muscle groups involved large or small?* All these elements can influence the power of a kick, so they all required some consideration and scrutiny.

When the NFL footballer kicked the ball, it did travel a good distance, but the kick seemed to come almost exclusively from the knee. This meant there was minimal large muscle group involvement except for the quadriceps. The NFL footballer dropped the ball, extended his leg by tensing his quadriceps, and shifted his hip forwards slightly so the core muscles were partially incorporated into the kick. Overall, the kick looked weak (compared to a martial arts kick), so I did not feel it would perform well on the power front. This led me to rating the NFL footballer's kick as a weak contender.

The Muay Thai fighter on the other hand was intimidating. As we saw earlier in the book, the way a Muay Thai round kick is thrown forces the body to incorporate many large muscle groups. The legs, core, arms, and even rotational torque are thrown into the kick to maximise its potential for devastation. Upon impact, the bag boomed as it was struck and echoed around the room hauntingly. It was a mightily impressive kick and I thought it would be difficult to beat.

After this, the footballer was assessed. The ball sat patiently on the penalty spot waiting to be kicked. The footballer readied himself, worked out his distancing, and began to sprint towards the ball. In his defence (and you know I don't like football) it was a reasonable kick. It looked a little like the NFL kick but with more hip incorporation, making it appear slightly more powerful. It didn't look to be a patch on the Muay Thai kick, but it wasn't bad given it had been thrown by a fragile, injury-prone, soft-as-they-come footballer who was later startled by a fluffy puppy and knocked over by a slight breeze on his way home.

Next on the list was the Capoeira fighter. As mentioned before, I was unsure as to what to expect from the mighty Martelo de Negativa kick. All I knew was that if the kick lived up to its name, then this was a one-horse race. Capoeira is such a rhythmic, fluid style, it can be hard for an untrained eye to pick out and break down all the movements involved. The first thing that caught my attention was that he was starting the kick by half lying on the floor! He placed both feet and his right hand on the ground whilst leaning backwards into a sort of low, collapsed tabletop position. From there he steadied himself whilst focusing intently on the bag that sat in front of him on a giant rocking spring. From that position he threw his left leg out straight into what looked like a breakdancing move, which appeared to me to be for the purpose of generating torque and incorporating the abdominal muscles. His body was then rotated releasing the pent-up torque so that his right leg flew over the top of his left that was now positioned on the ground for balance. His right leg arched across his centreline, much like the Muay Thai round kick, and struck the bag with the thunderous crack. The bag rocked like it had been hit by a car. I was impressed. All of this caught me by surprise. I was even thinking that this kick may challenge the Muay Thai round kick. I was no longer certain of myself. Once the bag had stopped rocking the other martial artists looked at one another in astonishment. Probably much like me, Capoeira was quite significantly off their radar, so its powers, tricks, and destruction were hidden amongst its seductive looking moves. I can tell you one thing witnessing this kick did to me, though. It made me certain I never want to be kicked by a Capoeira fighter.

It was now the turn of the Karate fighter. His choice of a front kick still baffled me, but he was a 7th degree black belt and I'm out of shape and easily confused so I kept my premature judgement to myself. With his crisp white Gi bottoms and jet-black black belt he stepped onto the platform and eyed the bag. Much like a Karate demonstration, he found a stance and steadied himself in preparation to strike. The bag now sat still in anticipation of pending impact.

The scientist from the sideline gave a count down, '3...2...1...' and the Karate fighter launched his rear leg towards the bag like a bullet. Upon impact the bag began to rock wildly, but the kick didn't seem to have possessed the power of the Muay Thai and Capoeira kicks. He utilised good technique and struck the bag with the ball of his foot with his toes pointed back. He also hit through the bag to ensure the energy of the kick travelled entirely through the object as opposed to just to it, which is good form for maximising striking power. Hitting *to* an object as opposed to *through* it is a sure way to significantly reduce the power of a strike, as the power contained diffuses on the surface of the object as opposed to travelling through it. A good way to think of this is by imagining hitting a watermelon with a baseball bat. Given the opportunity you would obviously want to smash the watermelon to pieces in a spectacular display. So to do this, *would you swing the bat towards the watermelon and stop it immediately upon impact? Or would you smash the watermelon to pieces by swinging the bat all the way through it?* Of course, the latter is what we would all do. The same principle applies to striking in martial arts. The front kick was great. It was a technically well thrown kick that I wouldn't like to be on the receiving end of, but didn't seem to compete with the others.

Lastly, the Taekwondo fighter stepped forward. As we know already, his kick of choice was the round kick. Upon being summoned he leapt onto the platform cockily. As you know, wasn't sure his kick choice was the best either, because it felt like he was competing against the Muay Thai fighter on his rule Regardless of my opinion, the fighter took his position like all the martial artists before him and awaited his instruction to strike. On the countdown was complete and he felt ready, he threw a kick that could only be described as moving at the speed of a lightning bolt. One second his right foot was on the floor, and a split second later the bag was swinging like crazy, and his foot was back on the ground again. At this moment I thought of the previously discussed equation: *speed* + *strength* = *power* and concluded that this was rather spectacular kick. The speed was incredible, and he was in good shape too, so it looked like he also had a fair amount of strength to insert into the kick. But his technique looked a little odd. Firstly, he didn't throw his kick in the way I knew Taekwondo fighters tend to – it looked like he used more of a Muay Thai round kick technique to me. Secondly, he jumped slightly so his bodyweight was off the floor at the moment of impact. Now I was even more confused. I was sure the Muay Thai fighter would have the most powerful kick, but the Capoeira and Taekwondo fighters had caused me to rethink.

So, my prediction from weakest to strongest was this: NFL footballer, Footballer (Soccer), Karate, Taekwondo, Capoeira, Muay Thai.

What do you think?

The real answer:

NFL footballer – the kick struck the ball with 91kg of force.

Footballer – the kick struck the ball with 114kg of force.

Karate – the kick travelled at 71mph and landed with 195kg of force.

Muay Thai(!) – the kick travelled at 130mph and landed with 635kg of force.

Capoeira – the kick travelled at 99mph and landed with 816kg of force.

Taekwondo(!) – the kick travelled a 136mph and landed with 1,043kg of force!

This astonishing data shows that the Taekwondo fighter landed a kick with almost 1,000kg more force than an NFL football player. That is unbelievable.

If you ever doubted the efficacy of martial arts, now is the moment to repent.

HOW HARD CAN YOU KNEE?

For those of you who've never trained in martial arts, it's most likely you will understate the devastation a knee strike can cause. Most untrained martial artists focus predominantly on punches due to the prevalence of Boxing in the combat sports arena. Mixed Martial Arts is rapidly challenging this hegemonic belief system, however, and the likes of knees, elbows, and ground fighting are working their way into the minds of non-martial artists and combat sports spectators worldwide.

From an outside perspective, an individual may ask *why knee somebody when you can punch or kick them? Surely a knee strike is less powerful than a kick, and therefore less effective?* From the perspective of a non-trained martial artist this line of thought is understandable. Understandable, but wrong. The reason this line of thought is wrong is because different techniques are more or less effective at different times. There is also more to impact power than how fast a limb is moving or how powerful somebody's muscles are. Other aspects such as kinetic linking (which we have already explored) muscular torque, timing, body position, the strike's endpoint, muscular incorporation, and the manipulation of your opponent's body can all be factored into the equation of how effective and damaging a technique can be. And through the intelligent manipulation of these points, a knee strike can prove to be one of the most devastating strikes available.

This statement doesn't take much to prove. All you need to do it watch a few good Mixed Martial Arts or Muay Thai fights and you'll see the true efficacy of a knee strike in action. A knee strike to the solar plexus can wind and down an opponent instantly. A knee strike to the side of the body can crack ribs and cause organ damage.

As for a strong knee strike to the face, well, this requires no explanation.

It's also important that we don't purely focus on power and impact. Although that is the point of this section, as it adds a dash of colour to the arts while allowing them to be quantified, there is much more to a martial arts technique than power. My aim here is not to show you which technique is the most powerful but to show you how powerful each technique can be. A less powerful technique utilised at the right time will always beat a more powerful technique used at the wrong time. It may well be true that a knee strike is not as powerful as a kick (we will find out shortly), but there are moments in a fight where a kick will not suffice but a knee strike will. Imagine trying to kick your opponent whilst they're holding your head. You would soon learn you are too close to land (or even throw for that matter) a good kick that will cause any damage. But in this exact situation a knee strike would be in its element. It's sharp, fast, deceitful, and perfect for close quarter combat. I hope this shows that it's not as simple as picking the most powerful technique and relying on it. It's vitally important to understanding each technique for what it is and apply it in the correct situation. That is the route to victory.

Now my preamble is over, let's get back to the question in hand: *how hard can you knee?* The art most famous for its knee strikes is Muay Thai. Muay Thai is commonly termed as the science of eight limbs because it uses eight parts of the body to strike with: hands, elbows, feet, and knees. Muay Thai is not alone in this, however, as many other arts also utilise knees as part of their arsenal. But as Muay Thai is the most famous of these arts, it will be our focus to help answer our question.

As part of a scientific experiment to help discover how hard a Muay Thai fighter can knee, a rather concerned looking crash test dummy is placed on a stand and linked up to an impact registering system. From the offset it's easy to feel bad for the crash test dummy. The Muay Thai fighter's legs are bulging with muscle and

145

look as solid as tree trunks. It's clear to see he's been practicing the art for many years, which appears to have turned his body into some type of wrecking machine. Muay Thai fighters are known for kicking down banana trees and kicking through baseball bats, so it seems to me he's not the type of guy you want to mess with. Not only this but he's also wearing electric-blue shorts, which I'm thinking he may have chosen because they help his legs move faster. He clinches the dummy by placing the palms of his hands on the back and top of its head, whilst squeezing its head on either side with his forearms. He narrates what he's doing for the benefit of the observing scientists. As he grabs the dummy's head, he explains, 'I'm gona pull the head down, get it at the right angle [he sets up his foot positioning with his left leg in the lead and his right leg at the rear], and from here, right to the sternum [he slowly lifts his right knee towards the dummy's sternum to show what he plans to do], then I'll bring it back after I've pulled the head right into it'. He slowly demonstrates the knee strike a few times whilst getting familiar with the way the dummy moves in his clinch. Once he's happy he steps back from the dummy and bounces easily on nimble toes. He openly admits he has never had the power of his knee strike tested before, but from professional fighting experience he claims, 'if you take a knee right to the sternum, you're out. That's it. Cracked ribs'.

The scientists finalise their preparation and once they're happy everything is working as it should, he's given the go-ahead to knee the dummy with everything he has.

The dummy sits perfectly still facing him for a moment in what feels like a midday western showdown. Then, in what looks like an almost casual moment, the fighter seamlessly glides toward the dummy, grabs the back of its head with his right hand and the back of its neck with his left, and throws a quick, sharp knee towards its chest. He abruptly exhales on impact as his knee sinks into the dummy's chest, before releasing the dummy and stepping backwards into the position he started in. As a knee strike is short

146

and fast with a small impact point, there is no loud bang to register its landing, nor a devastating looking collision that makes you recoil in shock. Just a wincingly painful looking stab to the chest. This is part of the reason knee strikes are so effective. They incorporate a lot of muscle and torque, your opponent's body is simultaneously pulled into the strike when it lands which increases the force of impact, and the impact area is small meaning all generated force is highly concentrated with very little opportunity to dissipate.

A bearded and bespectacled scientist watches the computer screen in anticipation of the results. A sensor in the dummy's sternum has captured two measurements: force (the strength of the blow) and compression (how far the knee strike has driven the ribcage back into the body compressing its innards). After a brief wait, the results are in. One of the scientists looks to the fighter and says, 'what you generated were numbers we see in a 35mph car crash'. According to the online Omni Calculator created by Dominik Czerina, PHD, a 35mph car crash for an individual weighing 70kg and wearing a seatbelt hits you with an impact force of 4,367kg. That's an unimaginably painful knee strike. The results also show the strike compressed the dummy's chest by almost two inches, which is sufficient to cause cracked ribs, internal bleeding, and organ and nerve damage.

I wonder how powerful his knee strike would have been had he not been wearing his blue shorts.

HOW EFFECTIVE ARE GRACIE JIU JITSU SUBMISSIONS?

So far in this section we have focused exclusively on strikes. We've seen that being kneed in the solar plexus is comparable to a car crash, a kick can land with an impact of over 1,000kg, Bas Rutten can puncture your spleen in a single punch (don't mess with Bas) and with training you can strike faster than a snake. All very cool

147

stuff. But as we know, striking within the martial arts is only part of the game. So, now I feel it's time we took a look at grappling.

For the sake of our grappling investigation, we will focus on the incredibly popular art of Gracie Jiu Jitsu (GJJ). GJJ is undeniably a fantastic art that has challenged and changed the landscape of modern-day martial arts forever.

It would be fair to say that the combatively effective martial arts as a whole are better thought through and more intelligently applied than almost all non-practitioners imagine. To an outside spectator, the *art* of the martial arts is often invisible. Most untrained individuals usually only see a barrage of random strikes being thrown, and when the fight hits the ground, they watch what looks like two people randomly rolling around trying to either stand up or get on top of each other. This could not be further from the truth; especially in the world of GJJ.

In my opinion, GJJ has taken the world by storm for one simple reason: efficacy. The efficacy of GJJ is evident in its saturation of martial arts and popular society. It didn't become popular because it looks good in movies or had a well-funded marketing campaign. It became globally recognised because proved itself on the world stage, under pressure, time and time again. With its ways, GJJ has joined an elite group of arts that place a predominant focus on technique over speed, strength, or power. Sure, speed, strength and power are always welcome allies in the arts (just take a look at the physical condition of modern-day G competitors if you don't think physicality matters in the art), but the art's laser-like focus on timing, leverage, physics, and chess-like intelligence allows it to be successfully used against stronger, faster, more powerful opponents who don't possess as much knowledge you do. GJJ is not unique in this regard. Wrestling and Judo are very similar in their approach. But it's a superb way to approach combative situations – especially for smaller individuals who want to learn the skills to protect themselves against often larger, stronger, more intimidating opponents.

GJJ takes the application of timing and leverage and applies it to all aspects of the art. If you're in a bad position on the ground and want to escape or move to a more advantageous position, then timing and leverage are used to help you achieve this. Techniques such as knocking your opponent off balance so you can tip them to one side or waiting for them to shift their base so you can monopolise on the weak point in their structure are used. The same is said if you want to submit, or in real combat, seriously injure your opponent. Timing and leverage are used to manipulate, dislocate, and break joints, or choke someone unconscious. The art's nickname 'human chess' is well earned. Many serious GJJ practitioners think many moves ahead and intentionally force set reactions from their opponents by leaving traps or making fake moves. It's for these reasons and more that I would say GJJ is one of the most intelligent arts out there and should form part of all martial artists arsenals.

But how effective are GJJ submissions? What can you achieve by manipulating the body by forcing it to move in a way it's not supposed to? We cannot investigate every GJJ submission here as there are simply too many – you'd be surprised how many ways there are to twist, choke, and break a body. So, we will focus on a single joint manipulation submission which is a neck crank from a position called *the crucifix*. However, what we will see when we look at this neck crank submission will be applicable to all joint submissions, whether it's a straight arm bar, kneebar, or kimura. The application of leverage and physics forcing a joint to move in a way it's not designed to, or move beyond its evolved range of motion, will provide similar results.

Although a neck crank from the crucifix is not the most common of GJJ submissions, it does have the advantage of allowing you to temporarily feel like Jesus before getting your neck broken.

There are a couple of different crucifix positions in GJJ, but the one we will focus on for now is when you are lying on your back underneath your opponent's upper back at 90 degrees to their

149

body. You would have one of your opponent's arms trapped by your legs and the other trapped by your upper arm.

The person demonstrating this submission on the *Fight Science* documentary is the legend, Rickson Gracie. Rickson is famous throughout the GJJ world not just because he's a Gracie, but because he's coined as being the best GJJ fighter of all time.

Rickson stands on the mats of the studio in a crisp white Gi and black belt. His belt is littered with stripes denoting his skill level in Gracie Jiu Jitsu. He truly is a man you wouldn't want to mess with. He speaks for GJJ practitioners as a whole when he says, 'the ground is pretty much home for us. I want to get close to my opponent and once I'm close I can either go to your body, to your legs, or even to your head. Then once I'm here and I take you to the ground, you're in my territory'.

The scientists place a dummy on the mats. Its neck is crammed with load cells which can measure the tension, compression, flexion, and extension of the neck. Rickson slips under the back of the dummy like he's shuffling under a duvet. Once in position, he traps the dummy's far arm with his legs and its close arm under his upper arm. The dummy now looks like a bald, beardless Jesus in blue overalls, with Rickson's body acting as the horizontal beam of the wooden cross. The scientists let Rickson settle into position then begin to count down, '3...2...1...'. On '1' Rickson grabs the dummy's head covering its right ear with both hands and pulls. You can hear the dummy's neck crack as he uses his leverage to crank the head towards him and almost off the shoulders. Just hearing the crack of the neck and seeing the angle of the head makes me wince at the thought of this technique being applied for real. Rickson manages to pull on the dummy's head with such force that the load cells in the neck record 272kg of lateral force. That's sufficient force to break the neck and paralyse the human body.

The dummy, considering it's just had its neck cranked by one of the world's greatest fighters, looks unfazed. But I wouldn't be surprised after the way the neck was cranked if the scientists have a rather substantial repair bill. I hope they have dummy insurance. Either way, what was showcased by Rickson and recorded by the scientists was a very grim but soberingly real display of the capabilities of GJJ.

7

THE FUTURE OF MARTIAL ARTS

'The future depends on what you do today.'

Mahatma Gandhi

When someone speaks of the future, it must never be taken too seriously. This book is no different. If we could accurately predict the future, the spark, vigour, and beauty of our lives would be extinguished. Knowing the future would dilute the present and trouble our minds. It's obvious to say the future is a mysterious place where anything is possible. A place where our hopes and dreams reside, and the loom of darkness and fear lurks. It's the unknown section of the path we precariously walk together. The mere act of speaking of the future is inherent with risks, as it's easy to ridicule someone for their opinions about what will happen and what shape the world of the next generations will take. It's easy to believe their predictions and interpretations are misguided and based on bad knowledge and experience. And it goes without saying that it's far easier to be wrong than right when making guesses about what is to befall us all.

The reason for this is because there are almost infinite paths the future could take, of which only one will be walked by civilisation. This means the chance of us accurately predicting the right path by analysing the available information of the present is almost impossible. There is a theory that at some point in the future we will be able to predict the future. This ironic prediction of a prediction is based chiefly around Newton's third law of motion which states, 'for every action there is an equal and opposite reaction'. The simple premise of this idea is that if we know the current action being taken in intricate detail (most likely through the real-time harvesting of billions or trillions of data points) then we can predict what that action's 'equal and opposite reaction' will be. Achieving this would require a currently unfathomable amount of computational processing power, and a rather large dose of super-intelligent artificial intelligence. Neither of which I happen to have to hand. But, as simple and appealing as this idea seems, it has many opponents. This is because the variability involved in such a prediction (the further away you travel from the initial action the more complex the equations become) is considered too large, even for a highly intelligent, dashingly charismatic supercomputer. *So, what chance do I have?*

But, even if we don't predict the correct path, if we are lucky, it may be possible to guess the rough direction and approximately where it will lead us. This is a much more realistic pursuit than trying to accurately predict what will happen overall and could be considered less of a prediction and more of an orientation. But even an attempt to orientate and not predict is fraught with almost guaranteed errors. Trying to orientate us towards what we think the future will hold is a volatile and risky business. In our efforts to try and guess what will happen we'll be called dumb, naïve, and ill-informed. But, for the sake of controversy and conversation, I'm willing to put my neck on the line and say I think the future of martial arts will be strongly influenced by the following five points: new and evolving technology, the emergence of the unknown unknowns, inter-disciplinary practices and collaboration, money, and a deeper exploration and understanding of human limits. I will also delve into each of these points in more detail to proffer my opinion on why I think they will prove influential to the future of martial arts.

TECHNOLOGY

I feel this is an easy one, almost a copout. If you ask anybody about the future of anything, the term *technology* will likely be spoken within the first 30 seconds or so. Technology, in all its glory and power, is undeniably ubiquitous. Technology has helped shape, develop, strengthen, and improve life for pretty much every single person on this planet. From the stone tipped spears of the hunter-gatherers of yesteryear, to the facial recognition software of today technology has played a significant role in the development of society. It helps to heat our homes, cook our food, assist with transport, and provide us with entertainment. It has even helped shape this book as I sit here now typing on a laptop and undertaking research. If you're reading this on a Kindle or e-reader, then technology is aiding you in accessing your books. Even if you're reading this as a physical book, the cover design, typeface, printing and binding have all been achieved through the targeted use of technology. Technology is inescapable in today's world, so I feel I would be irresponsible to dismiss its role in shaping the future of martial arts.

Technology is so interwoven with society that it already influences every single aspect of martial arts today. From training mats and uniforms to sports supplements and physical therapy technology has influenced and helped develop it all. So, in my mind it would be physically impossible for martial arts to escape the auto catalytic nature of technology, as to do so would require the undoing of society.

In Daniel E. Lieverman's book, *Exercised,* he argues that biological and cultural evolution are inseparable. This is because technology improves and evolves, the way a society functions also changes. Then, as the way a society functions changes, the human body biologically adapts to its new, technologically altered environment. Liberman uses the example of a chair to help prove this theory. Before the invention of chairs, people would either squat, kneel, or sit on the floor unsupported. These sitting techniques helped keep a person's back and legs strong as they were the parts responsible for maintaining stability and posture. But when the chair was invented, people began to shun the old ways of sitting and positioned themselves on seats because they were more comfortable. This mass adoption of chairs over squatting and kneeling has led to the tightening of calves, a loss of flexibility in the hips, and the weakening of the lower back – hence the western world's backache epidemic and the universal presence of back supporting office chairs.

If this theory is true, and I personally struggle to find fault with it, then it shows the evolution of technology is intricately linked to the evolution of everything, including martial arts. This makes me believe that as technology evolves, martial arts will too as a by-product.

In the future I strongly believe that training methods will improve through the use of applied data. Data, which at the time of writing is the most valuable asset on the planet, holds massive potential for revolutionising martial arts in ways we can currently not imagine. An example of how data may change the landscape is through greater scientific analysis that will make training more unique to the individual, allowing them to train in a more tailored manner, and therefore bolstering performance in ways that were previously impossible. Apps will be developed that allow the average person to analyse their biomechanics, brain speed, muscular function, and thought patterns in a detailed and holistic way. Your body size and shape could be calculated to help determine what the best martial art, or combination of arts, is for you. Algorithms may help shape your training so it's of most benefit to you, allowing you to monopolise on the techniques and movements that are most suited to your age, fitness, flexibility, intelligence, personality, and goals. And if you provide these apps and systems with sufficient data, they will be able to accurately predict how you will develop as a martial artist and have training plans and techniques pre-calculated for your continuing development. Aspects of these technologies already exist, as I am sure many of you are aware, but they are very much in their infancy and there is vast scope for improvement. My prediction is that they will become slicker, faster, more accurate, effective, and available. This is by no means a ridiculous prediction, however, as these things are an inevitable by-product of the auto-catalytic nature of technology. Technology always improves, refines, and changes, fuelled by the inquisitive nature of the human mind. And as it does, martial arts will be along for the ride.

If we speculatively pushed further into the future, then I believe it would not be unreasonable to predict the emergence of bioengineering. This could arise as the implanting of chips into the human body to improve performance or the accuracy of data collection, the linking of the mind with a machine allowing quicker learning, better information retention, and improved creativity, or the uploading of knowledge to the human brain to allow someone to gain the benefits of experiences they've never had. Attempting to make predictions that reach so far into the future is a risky business, because as we learnt above, the further you drift from the present day the more complex the calculations become and the margin for error increases drastically. It's often said, however, that science fiction is a precursor to science fact. So, these predictions may not be as wild as they seem.

Depending on your outlook in life, the above paragraph may make you squeal with joy, or recoil in horror. The integration of human and machine is a vastly controversial topic, which from my perspective, seems almost inevitable.

To help strengthen my case, Elon Musk has publicly said he believes we are all cyborgs already. As crazy as this sounds on the surface, his explanation does make one think. His reasoning is that we all carry a smartphone with us, and we use that phone to record our thoughts, converse with friends and family, track our movements, and answer questions we don't know the answers to. This means our smartphones act as an extension of our mind and capabilities. They allow us to know more, communicate further, and record things that the human body alone could simply not do. On the basis of this he claims we are already integrated with machines; we just don't realise it. This means the next step in technological evolution is likely to be greater integration between human and machine. From my perspective this line of thinking makes logical sense, and the more integrated with technology we become, the more blurred the lines between what is biologically real and what is technologically augmented become.

Essentially, we are trapped in a technological arms race. This is evidenced today by the levels of doping we see in major sporting competitions. Many world-class athletes are already trying to gain an advantage through the use of performance enhancing drugs. *What makes you think the same thing wouldn't happen if people had access to powerful performance enhancing technology?* Imagine you're training in martial arts and everyone in the class is technologically augmented except you. This could mean you lose every fight, are slower, clumsier, and weaker than everyone else, and do not learn the movements, techniques, and curriculum as quickly as the new starters. You would feel deflated and inadequate in your position as the worst martial artist in the class. Not only that, but if you were studying the martial art for self-defence, and you knew people on the street were technologically augmented too, then without embracing the onslaught of technology you would forever be on the back foot, fighting with a significant disadvantage in all combative situations.

So, what would you choose, technological augmentation or biological stagnation?

THE UNKNOWN UNKNOWNS

'There are the known knowns. These are the things we know that we know. There are the known unknowns. That is to say, there are things that we know we don't know. But there are also the unknown unknowns. These are the things we don't know we don't know' – Donald Rumsfeld.

Since Rumsfeld's poignant uttering in 2002, philosophical circles have lauded his 'unknown unknowns' statement with religious like zeal. The statement is a superbly apt illustration of the limitations of human knowledge, and how the gaps in our current knowledge may be perceived. Thinking of things in terms of 'knowns' and 'unknowns' also helps to paint the picture about how we should interpret modern day martial arts, and how we can acknowledge and address our uncertainties about the future of the arts themselves. The future of anything will inevitably contain a mixture of both unknows and knowns. There will be 'unknows' because that is the very nature of the future. But there will also be 'knowns' because almost nothing in this world happens purely by chance. The state of martial arts today is not a by-product of chance, it's the result of years of calculated development. The martial arts as we see them here and now are the result of years upon years of applied Kaizen philosophy.

Regardless of Rumsfeld's statement, however, it's very easy today to believe we have the martial arts figured out. Certain martial artists today practice their art with an unjustified feeling of martial superiority. They step onto the matts in the belief that martial arts are at their zenith. In the belief there is no further progress to be made, and that martial arts as a whole have been distilled into their most effective form. *And why would some people not think this?* Many martial arts are thousands of years old so there has been plenty of time and opportunity for development. They have been practiced and refined by millions of people via the shedding of blood, sweat, and tears. They've been integrated into one another, tested, refined, and honed into a plethora of highly effective fighting styles. And the current state of technology and globalisation has challenged, changed, and chiselled the martial arts into a global phenomenon practiced by innocent 4-year-olds (if there is such a thing), retirees, military personnel, and some of the greatest athletes on the planet. So, after all this, *how is it possible that we still have things to learn?* It's a great question, and one that I believe has two main strands to its answer. The first of which is due to the recency of globalisation and the newness of the true integration of global martial arts.

As we saw in previous chapters, martial arts (and martial artists) have been crossing borders and challenging one another for a long time. But, the global integration of all martial arts, each of which is competing for dominance on the world stage (we are not speaking of the conservative arts here that act as cultural vessels, but the arts focusing on maximal efficacy in combat) is a new thing which only really began in the 1980s or 1990s. This matters because in this global environment martial arts must learn to withstand threats from all other martial arts, as opposed to just one or two other arts, which would have been the situation previously encountered. Therefore, as an example, if Judo wished to claim superiority over all other arts, it would have to prove its dominance over all the striking and grappling arts we currently know of.

If we look at the global development of martial arts in this way, then we encounter our first unknown unknown pretty quickly. This is that not every martial art has yet gone global. The main arts are significant players in the development of the martial arts: BJJ, Muay Thai, Karate, Judo, Boxing, Taekwondo, etc. But there are most certainly arts out there that most people don't yet know exist, and these arts are one of our unknown unknowns. We don't know that we don't know about them. These arts may present new training methods, techniques, or variations on existing applications that the global community hasn't yet thought of. They could present new ways of pinning an opponent from side control, or more effective ways of generating punching power. We simply can't say. Some of you reading this may hoot at this suggestion, *but is this not exactly what happened when BJJ entered the global martial arts game? Did BJJ not change the way people perceived grappling and fighting?*

Before the introduction of BJJ, the guard position (lying on your back with your opponent between your legs) would have been laughed at as an offensive position. Now, people choose to adopt that position regularly (much to the confusion of many judokas and wrestlers), and they can cause a severe amount of damage to their opponent from it.

'But we have explored the world and discovered all the arts that matter!' You may shout. *Have we?* It's easy to believe we know everything and have seen it all by now, especially with how small modern-day technology makes the world feel, but I believe that's wrong. Yes, we have discovered, tested, and explored styles from a lot of places on Earth, *but how many arts can you think of that are present in today's global combat community that originated in Africa?* I imagine the answer is either none or very few. Africa is the world's second largest continent and second-most populous with roughly 1.4 billion people as of 2022, which accounts for circa 18% of the world's population. It's also the longest inhabited continent on Earth. Given this information, I think it would be irresponsible of us to overlook Africa as a potential source of untapped, high-quality martial arts and techniques.

The second strand that comes into play when trying to answer our question is that believing we have nothing left to learn requires us to lean on the naïve belief that the world never changes. If you are under the impression that the world doesn't change, then I have failed in my attempt at writing a convincing book on the evolution of martial arts. As we have seen already in the technology chapter above, biological and cultural evolution are inseparable. And cultural evolution is heavily influenced by technological development. This means as the world changes, which it ineluctably will, the requirements of our martial arts will change with it. This statement may not look correct if you only view it from a simplistic perspective, as you would rightly conclude that the purpose of martial arts has never really changed. The purpose of martial arts has always been to help an individual in combat. Although this true, it is too simplistic an outlook on how martial arts are utilised. Historically, most martial arts were designed to maim and kill. Today, martial arts are practiced more for self-defence, personal development, and fitness, than killing – except for military application. So, we can see that although the overriding purpose of martial arts has stayed the same (helping you in combat) the targeted outcome of most arts has changed – more self-defence, less killing.

The above shows that as the world changes, we will require different things from our arts than we do today, and at this moment in time it's not possible for us to say what those new things will be. This situation could be classed as a known unknown: we know martial arts will change, but we don't know how, when, or why. And the changes that do occur, and the knowledge that will fill the gaps that emerge as martial arts reshape themselves to meet our future requirements will be another batch of unknown unknowns. These unknown unknowns could be either new knowledge or reapplied old knowledge. We could discover something new that meets a future need we could not possibly have predicted, or we could revive a nugget of old knowledge that did not seem to meet the needs of the time but is a valid solution to a future problem. It simply isn't possible to say, but it is terribly exciting.

INTER-DISCIPLINARY

The mixing of disciplines feels like a modern invention, but this could not be further from the truth. With new terms like geoengineering, pharmacology, and bioethics being thrown around, it would be easy to conclude that only recently have we started to work together and approach subject matters holistically. But if you look critically enough you will see there are thousands of years of evidence showing we have combined disciplines to achieve our desired ends. The only difference between the past and present is we have now started to label our inter-disciplinary attempts so we can more greatly pinpoint, develop, and refine our attempts.

Inter-disciplinary application can be seen everywhere once you know what you're looking for, but for obvious reasons we will focus on martial arts. 'A Wrestling match is just physics' says Neil deGrasse Tyson, who in his younger years was the captain of his high school Wrestling team. 'Where is the tipping point? Where is the centre of mass? What are the support forces?' he questioned whilst he trained. I could not agree more with Tyson's explanation. This scientific approach to Wrestling is exactly the correct way to approach the art. But I feel his explanation does not just apply to Wrestling; it's applicable to almost every martial art. As we saw recently, BJJ efficiently uses applied physics to tip, trip, and submit opponents. Judo is the same. Knocking your opponent off balance or hijacking their centre of gravity so they can be thrown is Judo's bread and butter, all of which is achieved through the calculated, considered, application of physics.

It isn't just the grappling arts that utilise physics, however. Arts such as Muay Thai rely on physics to trip opponents, Kung Fu uses physics to deflect attacks using circular motions, and Karate uses physics to unbalance opponents making them vulnerable to attack whilst weakening their defences. As we saw at the beginning of this book, these arts have existed for a long time (especially Wrestling), which shows the disciplines of combat and physics have been interwoven for thousands of years. The reason this may have not been obvious before is because it has never been named, but if we labelled this inter-disciplinary approach 'physbat' (the physics of combat) then its prevalence will become obvious.

Other such examples are the use of strength and cardiovascular endurance training in martial arts. Strength training is a standalone discipline in its own right, as is cardiovascular endurance training. But for thousands of years these disciplines have been combined with martial arts to help create stronger, fitter, better fighters. Once again, this may seem obvious, but as these inter-disciplinary approaches have never been labelled, they are easy to overlook. We could call them 'strenbat' (strength training for combat) and 'cardibat' (cardiovascular endurance training for combat) if we wished to pin them down. Once labelled, these inter-disciplinary approaches will become disciplines in their own right. For example, physbat would not be the studying of physics as a singular discipline, which would then be twisted and forced to fit a martial arts model. It would be the targeted study of physics when fully applied to martial arts. This would make physbat a separate, hybrid discipline, with the sole purpose of maximising physics' applicability to martial arts.

This idea of inter-disciplinary application can be taken a step further. The discipline of biomechanics (the study of mechanical laws relating to the movement or structure of living organisms) is already an inter-disciplinary subject. But we can study biomechanics solely within the application of martial arts to help greater refine them. This has been happening for hundreds if not thousands of years already and the evolution of martial arts is evidence of this. As long as martial arts have been around, people have been scrutinising body positions and posture to help make martial artists as strong and effective as possible. Once again, this application of biomechanics to martial arts is known but has never been labelled as its own discipline. I will leave it to you to create whatever name you see fit.

If we are to look forwards instead of backwards, then we need to look to the future of martial arts and think about what new inter-disciplinary subjects there could be, or what currently existing inter-disciplinary subjects may be greater studied and developed for the benefit of the arts.

One example that springs to mind is that of nutrition. Sports nutrition already plays a large role in the development and performance of combat athletes and everyday people. But as research into nutrition deepens and becomes more specialised, its role in martial arts performance will become greater. As more is learnt about nutrition, and new and more successful ways of nourishing the body are developed, everybody from top level athletes to everyday individuals training in local sports halls will be able to apply this knowledge for their own performance gains.

Nutrition is a rapidly developing science and there is new knowledge emerging daily. As more is learnt about how the body reacts to nutrition, better advice and more effective diets will be devised which will enhance overall athletic performance and health longevity. I believe it's only a matter of time before nutrition leaps from being a general to a personalised science, where diets are tailored to each individual depending on their goals, genetics, existing health state, and reaction to certain macro and micronutrients.

At present, this lack of personalised nutritional data leaves entire populations open to poorly considered and outright dangerous nutritional advice. In the UK, the current state of nutritional advice is vastly flawed and often propagated by social media influencers and profiteering businesses. Many people follow fad diets such as the keto diet, which stigmatises carbohydrates whilst offering no real longevity. Protein is also worshipped as the most important nutrient, which comes with its own problems. Too much animal protein puts strain on the kidneys and increases blood acidity, which increases the chances of developing chronic kidney disease. As there is now too much acidity in your blood, your body, in an attempt to offset this increased blood acidity, must source calcium and put it into the bloodstream. As would be expected, the most available source of bodily calcium is to be found within the bones. If too much calcium is taken from the bones the likelihood of experiencing brittle bones and osteoporosis in later life increases. So, I would say it's worth understanding nutrition (or consulting a medical professional) before making drastic changes to your diet based on marketing campaigns and online advice.

Knowledge such as this causes many people to move to a vegetarian or vegan diet in the belief they are better caring for their health. But these diets come with their own pitfalls if you are not careful. A vegan diet is almost entirely devoid of vitamin B12, which must be supplemented in fortified form – all it takes is a quick Google search to learn what the horrific consequences of B12 deficiency are. And many foods sold that would form large parts of vegan and vegetarian diets are ultra-processed, making them extremely bad for your health.

Once nutritional advice becomes personalised and is reinforced by data, we can begin to shun the fad diets, poor advice, and ultra-processed foods for good. It will also make it much more difficult to be tricked by labels and big company marketing campaigns. There really is huge potential for the nutritional sciences to advance not just overall human health, but the performance and longevity of martial artists.

We could also consider the discipline of psychology, which seems to be everywhere these days. Psychology, much like nutrition, is already applied to combat sports and martial arts training under the name *sports psychology* or *mindset coaching*. But as our understanding of applied psychology deepens and its application to athletic and combative performance is refined, it seems logical that martial arts and psychology will become greater intwined to the benefit of both. Sports and performance psychology is used to great effect today and helps with such things as performance anxiety, confidence, emotional control, performance routines, flow states (achieving a state of mindless flow), goal setting, imagery, self-talk, and attention and focus. Imagine if you could increase your mental toughness, flow state, and performance through psychological training techniques that were ingrained throughout your martial arts curriculum. *What about increasing your likelihood of victory through tailored visualisation techniques, or increased emotional control and confidence through the use of a sports psychology app that learns about you whilst incrementally refining its recommendations?*

Given the potential in this area and this inter-disciplinary relationship, it seems to me that psychology will also become more personalised as opposed to generic, just like nutrition, and will proffer a whole series of training, performance, and mental advantages. Athletes are already using visualisation techniques today to help them attain victory, so this combination of disciplines is nothing new. But with a greater understanding of psychology and its applicability to the martial arts, I can only see its effectiveness increasing in the future.

It seems that when we speak of the inter-disciplinary nature of the future, and its effect on martial arts, the list of potentially influencing disciplines is endless. Progress in disciplines such as education, biology, and sociology will most certainly prove beneficial to martial arts if this progress is considered and applied intelligently. But we may also see benefits arise from development in less obvious disciplines such as manufacturing (new materials for Gis), fashion (new uniform designs), medicine (non-dangerous performance enhancing drugs), or climatology (maximally effective martial arts must change with their environment if they wish to remain relevant). Therefore, I would confidently proclaim that the better we work together in the future, the greater our influence on martial arts will be.

MONEY

Money may seem like a rather obscure addition to this list, but its powerful influence on the future of martial arts is evidently clear. It all comes down to one thing: commodification. Almost everything today is commodified, from coffee and sandwiches to TV and books. It would be nice to think martial arts have somehow managed to avoid this aggressive commodification process, but to believe that would be a lie. As we saw earlier, Miyamoto Musashi in the *Bo of Five Rings* called out martial arts commodification hundreds of years ago.

> *As I see society, people make the arts into commercial products; they think of themselves as commodities, and also make implements as items of commerce. Distinguishing the superficial and the substantial, I find this attitude has less reality than decoration. The field of martial arts is particularly rife with flamboyant showmanship, with commercial popularisation and profiteering on the part of both those who teach the science and those who study it.*

How many self-defence workshops have you seen available in your local area? What about the Gracie Academy which allows you to watch videos online, record yourself, upload your efforts, and receive belts and promotions if you perform well? What about martial arts being turned into sports? Certain branches of Brazilian Jiu Jitsu have become almost exclusively sports over the years, and certain aspects of Karate were combined and turned into Kickboxing many years ago. These are both examples of the commodification of martial arts. Commodification of martial arts is a very complex topic though, which we will not be able to cover in its entirety here. But in summary, it could be said that by commodifying the arts we are harming them with one hand whilst helping them with the other. Ironically, a real yin yang of a situation.

My outlook on the commodification of martial arts is not as bleak as Miyamoto Musashi's. I believe there is room for both the traditional arts and the sporting interpretations. They both serve different purposes and appeal to people for different reasons, as we have already covered earlier in the book. The issue arises, however, when the commodification of the arts creates a martial arts oligopoly, which ineluctably leads to the suppression of the lesser known, lesser funded arts, and the adoration of the better known, better funded arts.

As it is with most things we have covered so far in this section, this is not a new thing and has been happening for many years already.

Let's take a real-life example that is underway today. After the hype of Karate and Kung Fu in the 1970s had passed, the global martial arts scene faded away to nothing more than background noise. There were very few big, flashy martial arts gyms, and most instructors taught after work in sports halls and YMCAs. Then, one day, BJJ appeared and challenged all other arts to no-holds-barred fights. Since then, BJJ has gone from strength to strength by proving itself hardy, effective, and suitable for the smaller fighter. As BJJ became one of the world's most dominant martial arts it obviously gained many followers and converts from other arts. Ever since the birth of the UFC (which is a hyper-successful brand and promotional company based around the commodification of martial arts), BJJ has remained in the public eye whilst continually proving its worth under pressure.

Two things happened at this point, of which the order is crucial. Firstly, BJJ began to change. No longer was BJJ strictly a no-holds-barred street fighting art; it was changing its ways to meet the needs of sporting competitions and thus began to shun some of its more dangerous (illegal in competition) techniques. Secondly, due to these changes, BJJ became more successful in competition, which gave it greater credibility, more time in the limelight, and a larger following.

These days, sport BJJ and the original BJJ are considerably different. As I've said, I do not think this is a bad thing, but it does come with a problem. Due to the popularity of sport BJJ (which is what many schools now teach) the sport managed to infiltrate popular culture and become very rich.

The same happened years ago, albeit on a smaller scale, with other martial arts such as Muay Thai, Judo, and Karate. The end result of this process is that there are a small number of available arts making almost all the money in the market. And this process is self-fulfilling. The more money an art makes, the more it can spend on marketing, promotion, PR, fancy gyms, and sponsorship. This means the art attracts more students who bring with them even more money, which fulfils the cycle.

Hopefully you can see now that a martial art is no different from any other business. A supermarket works exactly the same, as does a restaurant or coffee shop. The reason all coffee shops sell pretty much the same coffees (lattes, flat whites, americanos, espressos, etc.) is not because they are all the coffees available, it's because they're what have been shown to be the most popular (and therefore most profitable) after much trial and error. Then, through the intelligent spending of profits, coffee shops such as Starbucks and Costa Coffee ensure they stay at the top of the game. That is until the game changes without them realising, or a new, surprise competitor arises in their blind spot and disrupts the market.

Money dictates who controls the market, to some extent, and once a martial art occupies the top spot and holds most of the money, it obviously wants to stay there. *And why would it not?* The instructors and gyms get rich, and many students have the opportunity to study and enjoy the art. It's a win-win situation for the art. But this drive to remain at the top of the game makes it easy for an art to become misguided and focus more on pleasing its practitioners (because it wants their money) and performing show-stopping fights in competition (to further perpetuate the art's popularity) than developing its true efficacy and spirit. As you will undoubtedly agree, this can cause an art to drift from the true martial path as it becomes a business first, martial art second.

If this happens and the art becomes more interested in profit than performance, its position will likely be usurped by another art. And if the new, usurping art is not careful, it may become tempted by profits and fall prey to the same destiny as its predecessor.

HUMAN LIMITS

*What stops us from physically pushing ourselves to death? And how
can we push ourselves a little bit closer?* These are the questions
Alex Hutchinson looks to answer in his superb book, *Endure*. In his
attempt to answer these questions he looks to sports industry
research and experiments to see what he can find. A very simplified
summary of his findings is that you can't exercise yourself to death
because your brain stops you. This sounds blatantly obvious, *but
what causes your brain to stop you? What mechanisms are
underway behind the scenes that inform the brain to slow things
down?*

Hutchinson explains that the limits of human performance
lie within six distinct areas: pain, muscle, oxygen, heat, thirst, and
fuel. If your body is in too much pain, then your brain will cause
you to stop exercising. This pain could be a by-product of lactic acid
build up, for example. The same is also said if your muscles are too
exhausted, you are lacking sufficient oxygen, your body
temperature gets too high, or that your body is running low on liquid
or fuel. All these things set off internal alarms that cause your mind
to act and prevent harm.

As we learn more about the human body and our
understanding of biology improves, we will be greater able to
manipulate these systems and increase human performance. We
could also look to the effect technology will likely have on human
performance. New electrolyte filled waters may be created that help
hydrate the body more effectively, or game-changing ultra-
processed foods that are light on the stomach, nutritionally dense,
instantly absorbable, and nutritionally complete may be devised.
Ways to instantaneously saturate the body with pure oxygen may be
developed, which will tackle the oxygen depletion issue head-on.
Real-time bodily function apps may be developed that track each of
the six performance limiting factors more closely and accurately
than the human brain is capable of, allowing individuals to push

themselves further, or to immediately address the factor that is limiting their performance mid-activity. Whatever route the development of technology takes, the only limit to its application will be the limits of our creativity.

This type of approach is only really applicable to top level athletes, however, as many everyday people never push themselves to the point of their true physical limits. *Have you ever pushed yourself to breaking point and been stopped by your brain before you overheated, collapsed of thirst, or simply found it too painful to continue?* Some of you may have, but the answer for most is likely not. I imagine others of you may think you have but have actually not. If I honestly ask myself this question my immediate answer is 'yes, I've had to stop because the pain my muscles were experiencing was too much'. But when I think about the question a little longer and compare what I've done to that of military personnel and extreme endurance athletes like free divers and ultrarunners, I quickly change my answer to 'no'.

I believe the achievable human limits (for both world-class martial artists and everyone else) will also be affected by each of the other four points we have discussed in this chapter. As we have already seen, technology will have a significant impact on what we are capable of. This point is so evident it's almost not worth mentioning. So will the unknown unknowns as we learn things we never knew or thought possible. Inter-disciplinary collaboration may help martial artists push past perceived pain barriers through the strategic use of psychological techniques; and hydration and fuel limits may be surpassed due to developments in nutritional science. Lastly, money will most certainly influence our human limits because technological advancement, research and development, and world-wide knowledge collaboration will not be possible without funding. Where that funding comes from is another matter, but there is one thing we can be sure of: the limits of human performance will likely be pushed in the direction that is most profitable and not most beneficial to the individual.

8

WHY MARTIAL ARTS?

'The ultimate aim of martial arts is not having to use them'.

Miyamoto Musashi

Martial arts have existed for millennia. As long as people have been fighting and falling out, fighting techniques have been used in an effort to help one defend oneself more effectively. But as Miyamoto Musashi said, 'The ultimate aim of martial arts is not having to use them'. This puts martial arts in a rather perplexing position. Imagine learning to play football but hoping to never have to play a real game. It would seem a waste. *Why bother learning football at all if you were never going to play it?* But, in my eyes, martial arts are not comparable with other physical activities as they are different in two rather distinct ways.

First of all, many people train in martial arts for the same reason they pay for house or car insurance. It offers them some form of protection should things go wrong, but they never hope to actually use it. Regardless of how confident you are in your combative capabilities, the potential for serious harm that comes with a real street fight far outweighs any desire to actually use what you have learnt in real life. The second thing is that martial arts are much more than a game or physical activity. They are a way of life. They are a means of self-refinement, a way to develop the mind, body, and spirit, and a portal to learning about the beauty of different culture. Yes, they teach you to kick ass and defend yourself if needed, but they also cause you to see the world differently. They teach you to effectively evaluate situations and respond to difficult times with more grit and flexibility than you would do without them

In a grappling match, you may put significant effort into gaining a certain position or setting someone up for a submission. Then, all of a sudden, your opponent moves or does something unexpected which ruins your plans. There is nothing to gain from complaining about the situation or getting aggravated that all the hard work you invested is wasted. You must simply accept the new situation, flow, and start again. This is very much the same in life. You may work hard, buy a house, get a promotion, and diligently grind to get your ducks in a row. Then, out of nowhere, you may lose your job or something unexpected happens that demolishes your perfectly built card tower. Of course, the pain experienced in such situations is very real, and the frustration experienced is genuine, but getting stuck in a state of anger and resentment because of what happened is of no benefit. You must improvise, adapt, and overcome. Martial arts teach you this.

Before I started training in martial arts, I was shy, weak, lacking confidence, and ugly. Now I'm just ugly. Martial arts taught me that real confidence is quiet, and that struggling with life is OK. Everyone does from time to time. They also taught me it's not about being the best person in the world at your chosen task but being the one that's doing it that matters. Hard work outperforms natural talent every time. As an example, there are many others in this world who are better placed than I to write this book. But the thing that matters is they're not writing it, I am. And within this lies my power. The power of grit, the confidence to take risks and fail, the tenacity to push myself outside my comfort zone, the knowledge that with applied Kaizen philosophy I can achieve more than I ever imagined. That is what martial arts have taught me.

There is also the rather depressing fact that martial arts will always be needed in this world. Aggression is part of human nature, so the ability to defend yourself will always be of importance. I'm fortunate to have never had to try and use my training in real life, but I know many who have. I don't want to. I never want to. I'd rather drink tea and read a good book. This is because I'm much more of a fan of the art than the martial, but as explained earlier in the book, I appreciate and acknowledge the requirement for both.

Not everything I have gained from my training is good, however, as martial arts have knocked my confidence in one large way. Before I started to train, I was under the impression that strength and size always won. I believed that the person with the biggest muscles was always the toughest. This meant I had confidence when being confronted by someone smaller or apparently weaker than I. But now I know this isn't true. I've been beaten up in MMA and Kickboxing by many people smaller, younger, and evidently weaker than me. I expressly remember receiving a good thrashing from a geeky looking 16-year-old who was built like a string bean. He was simply too fast, combatively intelligent, and technical for me. So, now I'm scared of everyone.

Thanks to the likes of the UFC, Pride Fighting Championships, ADCC, Karate Kombat, and K1, martial arts are back as part of popular culture. More and more people are taking up martial arts every year as their popularity continues to grow. This means many more people are benefiting from the improvements in physical and mental health they bring. And if you've never practiced martial arts before, I would encourage you to give them a try. It doesn't matter if you're eight or 80 years old, there's an art out there for you.

Getting into martial arts can be confusing because there are so many of them and they're all different. But my advice would be this. Take a look around your local neighbourhood and see what styles are on offer, as this will narrow down your options significantly. Then, search each of the arts you find on YouTube to see what they're all about. Most likely you will find Judo, Boxing, BJJ, Kickboxing, Karate, Kung-Fu, Muay Thai, MMA and Tai Chi clubs – there always seems to be a random Tai Chi class on a Tuesday morning somewhere. There are thousands of styles out there, but these are the most prevalent. Once you have decided which you like the look of drop the instructor a message (you will

174

normally get your first class free) and go along. I would also recommend you don't go along to watch the class – this is a sure way to get bored and never go back. Get involved and experience the art for yourself. You may find the art is perfect for you, but the instructor doesn't feel right, or vice versa, and that's fine. *Do you remember the equation we did early on in the book where you got one point for the art, one point for the instructor, and one point for you?* Think of your experience in this way. If you like the art but not the instructor, there is no shame in trying another school that teaches the same art. You're aiming for three out of three in your equation. Sometimes you may have to settle for two out of three, but if you can get three out of three you will go a long way in the martial arts community. Find a good club with a good instructor and put in the effort. You'll be amazed at what you can do.

Martial arts have been here a very long time, and I would say they're here to stay. You can find them in movies, TV shows, computer games, military training curriculums, the Olympics, books, and schools. They have truly saturated society and with good reason. They instil discipline, comradery, respect, commitment, work ethic, and creativity.

If everyone in the world studied martial arts, it would be a more peaceful place. This may sound oxymoronic. *How can teaching people martial arts possibly make them more peaceful? Is that not just teaching people to fight? Does it not make people more aggressive towards one another?* But it's true. Training, sweating, sparring, learning, and suffering with another person brings you closer together. It doesn't matter about their race, gender, salary, job, or beliefs. What matters is you're in this together. You have both committed your body and time to the pursuit of martial arts and that makes you family. You are there to help each other develop and learn. They allow you to use their body as a training device so you will be better equipped to defend yourself and your family if the need ever arises. If you were attacked or someone broke into your home and you successfully defended yourself and your family, you would be indebted to every person you ever trained with. Every instructor or fellow student who pushed you that extra mile or forced you to defend yourself from an uncomfortable position would deserve your thanks. Every single individual who had given up their time to allow you to train with them and develop your skills would be due your respect. Because without them and their commitment to your development, you may not have fared so well. *So, how do you thank them? How do you repay someone who is allowing you to use them so you can better protect yourself and your loved ones?* The answer: you offer your body in return. You give them your time and energy so they too will gain the ability to defend themselves and their family in a time of need.

That is the unspoken truth of martial arts.

Glossary of Terms

Armbar

An armbar is a technique used in many grappling arts where the arm is straightened and locked into position, sometimes with the aim to control your opponent, and other times with the intent to break the elbow joint. Today, the arm bar's most well-known application is within Brazilian Jiu Jitsu. The armbar can also be found within certain striking arts such as some styles of Kung Fu and Karate.

Boxing

Boxing is a fighting style that utilises only the hands to strike. A the time of writing, it is the most popular combat sport in the world

Brazilian Jiu Jitsu (BJJ)

Brazilian Jiu Jitsu, commonly known as BJJ, is a Brazilian martia art derived from Judo. The art rose to international acclaim afte being exported to the USA and is regarded, by many, as the be martial art in the world. It is a grappling art that relies strongly o using an opponent's strength and momentum against them.

Bushido

Bushido is the code of the samurai, which dictates the samurai attitude, behaviour, and lifestyle. The term Bushido is often used a catchall term for the codes, philosophies, and principles of samu culture.

Capoeira

Capoeira is a Brazilian martial art of African origin. The art is often practiced to rhythmic music and strongly represents a dance. Handstands, breakdancing like techniques, and large circuitous movements are all tell-tale signs of the art.

Cross (Punch)

A Cross is a straight punch thrown by the rear hand.

Fencing

Fencing is a French sword fighting art which is practiced as a sport. It is commonly seen in the Olympic games where the participants dress completely in white with a mesh covered face mask.

Front Kick

A Front Kick is a kick that travels straight down your centreline towards your opponent. It's fast, hard to see due to its direct line of travel and is found in many martial arts.

Gracie Jiu Jitsu (GJJ)

Gracie Jiu Jitsu (GJJ) is a martial art almost identical to Brazilian Jiu Jitsu (BJJ) but there is more focus on self-defence techniques and less focus on competition and sports fighting.

Grappling Arts

The grappling arts are those that orientate themselves purely around grappling techniques such as throwing, grabbing, ground fighting, and joint locking. Examples of such arts are Judo, Jiu Jitsu, Sambo, and Wrestling.

Ground and Pound

Ground and Pound is a fighting method used in Mixed Martial Arts (MMA) where the fighter uses grappling techniques to keep the fight on the ground, whilst throwing strikes at the opponent.

Guard Position

The Guard Position is a grappling position found in Brazilian Jiu Jitsu where the fighter lies on their back with their opponent between their legs.

Hook (Punch)

A Hook is most often a horizontally circular punch that can be thrown by both the lead and rear hand. Not all hooks are horizontal, as they are sometimes thrown at different angles. Regardless of the angle, a hook is always a circular punch that crosses the thrower's centreline.

Jeet Kune Do (JKD)

Jeet Kune Do (JKD) is a martial concept devised by Bruce Lee which focuses on the application of techniques and philosophies from any art or learning that best serves the individual.

Judo

Judo is a Japanese martial art that is derived from Japanese Jiu Jitsu. It's an Olympic sport and extremely effective form of fighting. Judo is typecast by two people trying to throw each other to the floor to score points.

Kali

Kali is the national martial art of the Philippines. The art places an emphasis on weapons-based fighting, such as swords, knives, and machetes. Due to the inherent dangers of training with such weapons, classically, Kali practitioners train with sticks made from rattan.

Karate

Karate is a Japanese martial art that focuses predominantly on striking – punching, kicking, hitting with elbows and knees. Some styles of Karate also focus on fighting with weapons, throwing, ground fighting, and locking joints.

Kata

A Kata is a set routine of techniques that can be practiced alone.

Kendo

Kendo is a modern Japanese martial art that uses bamboo swords and protective armour.

Kenjutsu

Kenjutsu is an umbrella term used for all Japanese swordsmanship.

Kickboxing

Kickboxing is an umbrella term used for sport versions of numerous striking arts. Kung Fu and Karate are two of the most famous arts that have branched into the sporting world and formed their own versions of Kickboxing.

Kung Fu

Kung Fu is an umbrella term used to describe many of the Chinese fighting arts. Typically, Kung Fu refers to the more traditional Chinese arts that focus predominantly on punching, kicking, and hitting with knees and elbows.

Luta Livre

Luta Livre is a Brazilian submission Wrestling combat sport. The art is a mix of Catch Wrestling and Kosen Judo, combined with striking.

Martial Art

A martial art is a fighting method that has been developed for both self-defence and self-offence purposes. Martial arts vary in their ways, ranging from punching and kicking, to grabbing, throwing, and locking joints, to using weapons such as knives, sticks, and swords. Some martial arts focus on just a single area (punching for example) and others focus on many areas (such as punching, kicking, and throwing). The aim of all martial arts is to enable their practitioners to be successful in combat.

Martial Concept

A martial concept is like a martial art, but it is willing to change its ways in the face of available evidence or individual empiricism. A martial concept aims to free its practitioners from hindering tradition and techniques in favour of personal preference and maximal efficacy. The aim of a martial concept is to create the most effective martial artist possible, not one who is limited by the constraints of a given art.

Mixed Martial Arts (MMA)

Mixed Martial Arts is a martial concept that involves the use of techniques from many different styles to defeat an opponent in a sporting environment that involves both striking and grappling techniques. Mixed martial artists are free to use techniques from any style they wish, as long as the techniques fall within the rules of the sport.

Mount Position

The Mount is a ground fighting position where one person is flat on their back and the other is on top whilst fully straddling them. The mount is known for being one of the most dominant positions in the grappling arts.

Muay Thai

Muay Thai is a striking art from Thailand. It is famous for its direct, no fuss, simple approach to combat. It is frequently regarded as one of the best striking arts in the world.

Ninjutsu

Ninjutsu is a Japanese martial art that focuses on the strategy and tactics of unconventional warfare. The art is steeped in mythology and is ironically famous for its secrecy. In popular history, the ninjas (a practitioner of Ninjutsu) were the arch enemy of the samurai. Classically, a ninja is depicted dressed completely in black from head to toe, with only a small slit in the hood for the eyes to see out.

No-Holds-Barred

No-Holds-Barred is a style of fighting with no rules.

Pankration

Pankration is an ancient Greek sport that combined Wrestling and Boxing.

Pentjak Silat

Pentjak Silat is an umbrella term used for many Indonesian martial arts. Pentjak Silat encompasses many styles that incorporate striking and weaponry in their arsenals.

Rear Naked Choke

The Rear Naked Choke is a submission found in many arts, but most famously in Brazilian Jiu Jitsu. The choke is applied by wrapping your arms around your opponent's neck from behind, which applies pressure to the arteries of the neck, cutting off the circulation to the brain.

Round Kick

A Round Kick is a kick that travels across your centreline, like that of the motion of a swung baseball bat. This kick is also known as turning kick or roundhouse.

Shooto

Shooto is a combat sport and mixed martial arts organisation formed in 1985. It is considered one of the world's first mixed martial art promoters.

Sidekick

A Sidekick is a kick that travels straight down the centreline toward your opponent with the toes and heel aligned horizontally with t hip turned over. This kick is thrown at all heights from the kneecap to the head.

Sprawl and Brawl

Sprawl and Brawl is a fighting method used in Mixed Martial Arts (MMA) where a fighter is skilled enough to stop their opponent's takedowns, keep the fight on its feet, and force their opponent into a striking match against their will.

Striking Arts

The striking arts are those that orientate themselves purely around striking techniques such as punches, kicks, knees, elbows, and headbutts. Examples of such arts are Boxing, Kickboxing, Lethwei, Muay Thai, Karate, and Kung Fu.

Taekwondo

Taekwondo is a South Korean martial art that relies heavily on high kicks. Its literal translation is 'the art of punching and kicking' and it can be found in the Olympic games.

UFC

The UFC (Ultimate Fighting Championship) is the biggest Mixed Martial Arts promoter in the world.

Vale Tudo

Vale Tudo is the frequently used Portuguese term for no-holds-barred fighting.

Wing Chun

Wing Chun is a style of Kung Fu devised by a woman – somewhat of a rarity in martial arts. It's also the style Bruce Lee originally trained whilst he lived in Hong Kong. Wing Chun is famous for its trapping techniques, which focus on manipulating your opponent's hands and arms by grabbing, slapping, and pinning them.

Yin Yang

Yin Yang is a Chinese philosophical concept that describes opposite but interconnected forces.

Bibliography

1. 2016. *Inner Engineering: A Yogi's Guide to Joy*. 1st ed. Harmony.
2. AFP, S.W.W. (2020). Palau Invites US Military to Build Bases as China Seeks Regional Clout. [online] The Defense Post. Available at: https://www.thedefensepost.com/2020/09/04/palau-us-military-bases/
3. andorrapartner.com. (n.d.). Andorra Army | Does Andorra Have a Military? [online] Available at: https://andorrapartner.com/andorra-military-army/#:~:text=Does%20Andorra%20have%20a%20militar y%3F%20In%20terms%20of
4. Arnold, D., 2015. Mushin: A Right-Brain State of Awareness that is the Artist within the Martial Artist. 1st ed. CreateSpace Independent Publishing Platform.
5. Assunção, M., 2005. *Capoeira*. London: Routledge.
6. BBC News. 2020. *Brazil's Capoeira Gets Unesco Status*. [online] Available at: <https://www.bbc.co.uk/news/world-latin-america-30219941>
7. Bishop, M., 1993. *Okinawan Karate*. London, Eng.: A & C Black.
8. BjjTribes. 2021. 13 of the best John Danaher quotes for BJJ and life - BjjTribes. [online] Available at: <https://bjjtribes.com/13-of-the-best-john-danaher-quotes-for-bjj-and-life/>
9. Black Belt Magazine, 1971. (Vol. 9 No, 9).
10. Black Belt Wiki. 2022. Mau Rakau - Black Belt Wiki. [online] Available at: <https://blackbeltwiki.com/mau-rakau>

11. Black Belt Wiki. 2022. Pradal Serey - Black Belt Wiki. [online] Available at: <https://blackbeltwiki.com/pradal-serey>

12. Blanchard, K., 1995. *The Anthropology Of Sport*. Westport, CT: Bergin & Garvey.

13. Boxing booth - BoxRec (no date). Available at: https://boxrec.com/wiki/index.php/Boxing_booth.

14. Brazilian Arts Foundation. 2020. *Capoeira History - Brazilian Arts Foundation*. [online] Available at: <https://brazilianarts.org/capoeira/capoeira-history/>

15. Brown, S., 2020. *A History Of Brazilian Capoeira*. [online] Culture Trip. Available at: <https://theculturetrip.com/south-america/brazil/articles/a-history-of-brazilian-capoeira/>

16. Calm.com. 2022. *Experience Calm*. [online] Available at: <https://www.calm.com/>

17. Capoeirauniverse.com. 2020. *Capoeira History – Capoeira Universe*. [online] Available at: <http://capoeirauniverse.com/capoeira-history/>

18. Clements, J., 2016. A Brief History of the Martial Arts: East Asian Fighting Styles, from Kung Fu to Ninjutsu. 1st ed. Robinson.

19. Contributors, W.E. (n.d.). High Protein, Low-Carbohydrate Diets. [online] WebMD. Available at: https://www.webmd.com/diet/guide/high-protein-low-carbohydrate-diets#:~:text=If%20you%20have%20any%20kidney%20problems%2C%20eating%20too

20. CostaRica.org. (2019). Costa Rica Military. [online] Available at: https://costarica.org/facts/military/.

21. Czernia, D. (2019). Car Crash - Impact Force Calculator - Omni. [online] Omnicalculator.com. Available at: https://www.omnicalculator.com/physics/car-crash-force.

22. Encyclopedia Britannica. 2020. *Wrestling | History, Styles, & Facts*. [online] Available at: <https://www.britannica.com/sports/wrestling>

23. Encyclopedia Britannica. 2021. Philippines - The Spanish period. [online] Available at: <https://www.britannica.com/place/Philippines/The-Spanish-period>

24. Encyclopedia Britannica. 2022. *Antaeus | Greek mythology*. [online] Available at: <https://www.britannica.com/topic/Antaeus>

25. FanSided. 2022. Here's a brief history of the UFC (1993-present). [online] Available at: <https://fansided.com/2020/03/20/casuals-guide-to-mma-a-brief-history-of-the-ufc-1993-present/>

26. Fight Science. 2006. [DVD] Directed by M. Stern. National Geographic.

27. Frantzis, B., 1998. *The Power Of Internal Martial Arts*. Berkeley, Calif.: North Atlantic Books.

28. Gachanja, N. (2021). The Roots of Capoeira Angola - Africa.com. [online] www.africa.com. Available at: https://www.africa.com/the-roots-of-capoeira-angola/

29. Gentry, C., 2004. No holds barred. Lytham: Milo.

30. Gomes, F., 2010. *Mocambos De Palmares*. Rio de Janeiro, RJ: 7Letras.

31. Google Books. 2020. *Humanities Dimension Of Physiotherapy, Rehabilitation, Nursing And Public Health*. [online] Available at: <https://books.google.co.uk/books?id=NY81p9dVI70C&=PA21&dq=Egyptian+paintings+showing+some+form+o+struggle+comparable+to+the+stocks&hl=en&sa=X&ei=zTOUYaTM8KsjAKBpoHIBw&redir_esc=y#v=onepage.q=Egyptian%20paintings%20showing%20some%20form

20of%20struggle%20comparable%20to%20the%20stocks
&f=false>

32. Google Books. 2020. *LIFE*. [online] Available at:
    <https://books.google.co.uk/books?id=gE8EAAAAMBAJ
    &pg=PA59&redir_esc=y#v=onepage&q&f=false>

33. Google Books. 2021. Tratado delos rieptos [et] desafios que
    entre los caualleros [et] hijos dalgo se acostu[m]bran hazer
    segun las costu[m]bres de España, Francia [et] Ynglaterra.
    [online] Available at:
    <https://books.google.co.uk/books?id=3CJ-
    57MPyTcC&pg=PT46&redir_esc=y#v=onepage&q&f=fals
    e>

34. Greger, M. (2019). How not to diet : the groundbreaking
    science of healthy, permanent weight loss. London:
    Bluebird Books Of Life.

35. Hallander, J., 1985. *The Complete Guide To Kung Fu
    Fighting Styles*. Burbank, CA: Unique Publications.

36. Harari, Y. and Ros, J., 2021. Sapiens. Barcelona: Debate.

37. Hatsumi, M., 2004. *The Way Of The Ninja*. Tokyo:
    Kodansha International.

38. Headspace.com. 2022. *Meditation and Sleep Made Simple -
    Headspace*. [online] Available at:
    <https://www.headspace.com/>

39. Higaonna, M., 1985. *Traditional Karate-Do*. Tokyo:
    Sugawara Martial Arts Institute.

40. Higaonna, M., 1987. *Traditional Karate-Do*.

41. Historyoffighting.com. 2020. *Karate*. [online] Available at:
    <https://www.historyoffighting.com/karate.php>

42. Hutchinson, A. and Gladwell, M., n.d. Endure: Mind, Body
    and the Curiously Elastic Limits of Human Performance.
    1st ed. HarperCollins.

43. Hyams, J., 1979. Zen in the Martial Arts. 1st ed. Bantam.

44. Imperial Combat Arts. 2020. *Rare Kung Fu Styles | Animal
    Substyles*. [online] Available at:

<https://imperialcombatarts.com/rare-kung-fu-styles--animal-substyles.html>

45. Jwing-Ming, Y. and Bolt, J., 1981. *Long Fist*. Hollywood, Calif: Unique Publ.

46. Kaizen.com. 2021. *What is KAIZEN™*. [online] Available at: <https://www.kaizen.com/what-is-kaizen.html>.

47. Kidadl.com. 2022. *100 Ultimate Martial Arts Quotes To Stay Zen*. [online] Available at: <https://kidadl.com/articles/ultimate-martial-arts-quotes-to-stay-zen>

48. Kingsford-Smith, A., 2020. *Disguised In Dance: The Secret History Of Capoeira*. [online] Culture Trip. Available at: <https://theculturetrip.com/south-america/brazil/articles/disguised-in-dance-the-secret-history-of-capoeira/>

49. Klingborg, B. and Lai, H., n.d. *The Secrets Of Northern Shaolin Kung-Fu*.

50. Knight Science Journalism @MIT. (n.d.). New study confirms that Africans are the most genetically diverse people on Earth. And it claims to pinpoint our center of origin. [online] Available at: https://ksj.mit.edu/tracker-archive/new-study-confirms-africans-are-most-gen/.

51. Kornfield, J., 2010. Meditation for beginners. Ahmedabad: Jaico Pub. House.

52. Lee, B., 2018. Tao of Jeet Kune Do. Oklahoma City: Black Belt Books.

53. Leonard, B. (1968). Karl Gotch, The Quiet Man, Speaks His Piece. [online] Puroresu Dojo. Available at: https://www.puroresu.com/personalities/gotch_karl/article.html

54. Leonard Lackinger, S., 2020. *The Five Animals Of Shaolin Kung Fu - Part 1*. [online] Shaolin-wahnam-wien.at. Available at: <https://www.shaolin-wahnam-wien.at/kungfu-5-tiere-1-en.php>

55. Levinson, D. and Christensen, K., 1996. *Encyclopedia Of World Sport*. Santa Barbara, Calif.: ABC-CLIO.
56. Lieberman, D., 2021. *Exercised*. [S.I.]: Knopf Doubleday Publishing Group.
57. Limalama.org. 2022. LimaLama®. [online] Available at: <http://www.limalama.org/> [Accessed 11 January 2022].
58. Maine News Online. 2022. *How Much Pressure To Break A Skull? - Maine News Online*. [online] Available at: <https://www.mainenewsonline.com/how-much-pressure-to-break-a-skull/>
59. Mendel, D. and Kerr, G., 1960. Okinawa. The History of an Island People. *The Western Political Quarterly*, 13(1), pp.436, 442, 448-449.
60. Mental Floss. 2022. *8 Little Known Facts About the Temple*. [online] Available at: <https://www.mentalfloss.com/article/502709/8-little-known-facts-about-temple>
61. Metmuseum.org. 2020. [online] Available at: <https://www.metmuseum.org/toah/hd/kana/hd_kana.htm>
62. Mindframe Performance. (n.d.). Mindframe Performance | Sport Psychology. [online] Available at: https://www.mindframeperformance.com/
63. Morgan, F., 2004. Living the Martial Way. 1st ed. Barricade Books, p.77.
64. MUSASHI, M., 2021. BOOK OF FIVE RINGS. [S.l.]: ARCTURUS PUBLISHING LTD.
65. Ninjutsu.org.uk. 2020. *The 18 Skills Of The Togakure Ryu Ninja*. [online] Available at: <http://www.ninjutsu.org.uk/the-18-skills-of-the-togakure-ryu-ninja.html>
66. Ninjutsu.org.uk. 2020. *History Of Ninjutsu*. [online] Available at: <http://www.ninjutsu.org.uk/history.htm> [Accessed 1 May 2020].

67. Nytimes.com. 2022. *The Martial Arts as Moneymakers (Published 1988).* [online] Available at: <https://www.nytimes.com/1988/08/28/business/the-martial-arts-as-moneymakers.html?scp=84&sq=chuck%20norris&st=cse>

68. Pankration.info. 2022. Total Combat Sport - Pankration - What is Pankration?. [online] Available at: <http://www.pankration.info/what-is-pankration/>

69. Pellaud, A., 2022. Freestyle Wrestling. [online] Web.archive.org. Available at: <https://web.archive.org/web/20120616221854/http://www.fila-official.com/index.php?option=com_content&task=view&id=33&Itemid=75&lang=en>

70. Peterson, J., Van Sciver, E. and Doidge, N., n.d. 12 rules for life. 1st ed.

71. Pickard, S., 2020. *The History Of Karate — Defense Arts Center.* [online] Defense Arts Center. Available at: <http://defense-arts-center.com/articles/2016/1/17/the-history-of-karate>

72. Polly, M., 2019. *Bruce Lee.* London [etc.]: Simon & Schuster.

73. Powell, G., 2020. Karate on a Cushion: A Journey into Zen. 1st ed. Independently Published.

74. Rice, M., 2002. *Who's Who In Ancient Egypt.* London: Routledge.

75. Sampson, K., 2022. 9 Things MMA Can Do Right Now to Replace Boxing as No. 1 Combat Sport. [online] Bleacher Report. Available at: <https://bleacherreport.com/articles/982565-15-things-mma-can-do-right-now-to-replace-boxing-as-no-1-combat-sport>

76. Sayokanfederasyonu.com. 2022. SAYOKAN DUNYA
    FEDERASYONU. [online] Available at:
    <http://sayokanfederasyonu.com/english/founder.htm>

77. Sherdog.com (no date) Vale Tudo: A Rich, Storied &
    Complex Past - Conde Koma and the Gracies. Available at:
    https://www.sherdog.com/news/articles/1/Vale-Tudo-A-
    Rich-Storied-Complex-Past-59571.

78. Shinobi Exchange | Ninjutsu. 2020. *History Of Ninjutsu
    And It's Evolution | Shinobi Exchange.* [online] Available
    at: <http://shinobiexchange.com/the-history-of-ninjutsu-
    and-its-evolution/>

79. Sherdog.com (n.d.). A Blood Called Shooto - Home Called
    Shooto. [online] Sherdog. Available at:
    https://www.sherdog.com/news/articles/1/A-Blood-Called-
    Shooto-17377

80. Spector, T. (2021) SPOON-FED : why almost everything
    we've been told about food is wrong. S.L.: Vintage.

81. Sterling, J., Jost, J. and Hardin, C., 2019. Liberal and
    Conservative Representations of the Good Society: A
    (Social) Structural Topic Modeling Approach. SAGE Open,
    9(2), p.215.

82. Steven Pinker, 2018. *Enlightenment Now.* Penguin Random
    House.

83. ThoughtCo. 2020. *The History Of Japanese Ninjas.* [online]
    Available at: <https://www.thoughtco.com/history-of-the-
    ninja-195811>

84. Tokyoezine.com. 2020. *The History Of Martial Arts In
    Japan.* [online] Available at:
    <http://www.tokyoezine.com/2011/04/27/the-history-of-
    martial-arts-in-japan/>

85. Traditionalsports.org. 2022. Bokator (Cambodia) -
    Traditional Sports. [online] Available at:
    <http://www.traditionalsports.org/traditional-
    sports/asia/bokator-cambodia.html>

86. Traditionalwingchun.com. 2022. History Chinese Martial Arts | Traditional Wing Chun KungFu North American Headquarters. [online] Available at: <http://traditionalwingchun.com/twckf/history-chinese-martial-arts/>

87. Trip, C., 2020. *The Historical Origins Of Karate*. [online] Culture Trip. Available at: https://theculturetrip.com/asia/japan/articles/the-origins-of-karate/

88. Turnbull, S. (2012). *The Samurai Invasion of Korea 1592–98*. Bloomsbury Publishing.

89. Tversky, A. and Kahneman, D., 1973. Availability: A heuristic for judging frequency and probability. *Cognitive Psychology*, 5(2), pp.207-232.

90. Ufc.com. 2022. Unified Rules of Mixed Martial Arts | UFC [online] Available at: <https://www.ufc.com/unified-rules-mixed-martial-arts>

91. Visit Vatican Info - Explore Rome with our Rome Travel Guide. (2021). Vatican City Population - Citizens & Army Population. [online] Available at: https://visitvatican.info/vatican-city-population/.

92. Walker, M., 2018. Why We Sleep: The New Science of Sleep and Dreams. London, UK: Penguin.

93. Web.archive.org. 2020. *Grapplingstyles*. [online] Availabl at: <https://web.archive.org/web/20150101053822/http://www kobukaijujitsu.com/grapplingstyles.html>

94. What-when-how.com. 2022. *Folklore in the Martial Arts*. [online] Available at: <http://what-when-how.com/martial arts/folklore-in-the-martial-arts/>

95. Worldometer (2019). Population of Africa (2019) - Worldometers. [online] Worldometers.info. Available at: https://www.worldometers.info/world-population/africa-population/.

96. Wta4u.com. 2022. What is Taekwondo? Where did the martial art originate? | World Taekwondo Academy. [online] Available at: <https://www.wta4u.com/taekwondo/traditional-taekwondo#:~:text=Taekwondo%20was%20developed%20during%20the,karate%20and%20Chinese%20martial%20arts.>

97. Wtokf.org. 2020. *The History Of Martial Arts*. [online] Available at: <https://wtokf.org/the-history-of-martial-arts.php>

98. www.youtube.com. (n.d.). Gracie jiu Jitsu. [online] Available at: https://www.youtube.com/watch?v=T82QDpy2DEo [Accessed 9 Nov. 2022].

99. www.youtube.com. (n.d.). muay thai melchor menor. [online] Available at: https://www.youtube.com/watch?v=oNhlDENU-Lk

100. Yang, J. and Bolt, J., 2000. *Northern Shaolin Sword*. Boston, Mass., USA: YMAA Publication Center.

101. Youtube.com. 2021. [online] Available at: <https://www.youtube.com/watch?v=NTk9V4TO1Fo&t=2510s>

102. Youtube.com. 2022. [online] Available at: <https://www.youtube.com/watch?v=UknX1Sp26ns>

103. Youtube.com. 2022. [online] Available at: <https://www.youtube.com/watch?v=cU4j-t2oYA0>

104. Youtube.com. 2022. [online] Available at: <https://www.youtube.com/watch?v=C2JhhzYqaB8>

105. Youtube.com. 2022. [online] Available at: <https://www.youtube.com/watch?v=qKsdLxxlgME>

106. Youtube.com. 2022. [online] Available at: <https://www.youtube.com/watch?v=LNfAwWk33nI>

107. Youtube.com. 2022. [online] Available at: <https://www.youtube.com/watch?v=maQINqPI7S0>

108. Youtube.com. 2022. [online] Available at:
    <https://www.youtube.com/watch?v=UZMIbo_DxJk>
109. Youtube.com. 2022. [online] Available at:
    <https://www.youtube.com/watch?v=8sSe6FSrylc>
110. 全日本剣道連盟 AJKF. (n.d.). 剣道・居合道・杖道.
    [online] Available at: https://www.kendo.or.jp/knowledge/

List of Figures

Acknowledgments

Firstly, as always, I would like to thank my beautiful wife, Roxana. Without her patience, tolerance, understanding, guidance, and advice, I would likely be a mere shadow of the man I am today. I cannot say how appreciative I am of you listening to me talk about martial arts (almost every day), and putting up with my endless ideas, rants, book questions, and daydreams.

I would also like to thank Isla, my daughter. Although you are only 10 months old at the time I write this sentence, you have already taught me more than I will ever teach you. You didn't contribute to this book in the slightest – you can't even speak. But writing a book on martial arts has been a long-held dream of mine, and I hope the mere existence of this book shows you that pursuing your dreams is a worthwhile endeavour.

It would be fair to say this book would not exist if it were not for the wisdom, experience, and teachings of my instructors and (some of) the students I've trained with. I would like to offer a special thanks to Mike Gregory who truly changed the way I look at martial arts.

I also couldn't write an acknowledgements section in a book of martial arts without mentioning David Ochwat. This book would likely have been much better if he hadn't punched me in the head so many times. If I get poor reviews, I'm blaming him.

Thank you to Jansen Yee for designing my book cover and promo materials. This book wouldn't look half as good if it wasn't for you. A special thanks also goes to Edward Eyer for contributing the stunning cover image.

Lastly, I would like to thank *you*, the reader. I am truly grateful for you taking the time to read *Punching Above Your Weight*. I hope you've enjoyed it.

Connect With the Author

liamdevonport.com

@LiamDevonportAuthor

Printed in Great Britain
by Amazon

34227943R00119